Ten Spurs

George Getschow, editor
Bill Marvel, associate editor

The Best of the Best
Literary Nonfiction of The Mayborn Conference
Vol. 7, 2013

ISBN 978-0-9786521-8-0

Contents

Foreword
by George Getschow

Bill Marvel, a very fine writer and associate editor of this publication, and I talk about the vagaries and vicissitudes of writing the way most people carry on about the weather. We talk about the constant fluctuations in form, style and substance, about the rise and decline in popularity of memoir, essay, biography and other genres among the reading public, about how the Digital Age has ignited tremors and aftershocks across a wide terrain of traditional publishing.

But a few weeks ago, Bill really got me thinking about an aspect of writing that I've never thought about before: the absurdity of what we do and how we do it. Just imagine, Bill said, if some creature from another planet landed on your lawn, knocked on your door and asked you what you do for a living.

"I'm a writer," you would say.

"What does a writer do?" the creature would ask.

"Well," you would say, "we hole ourselves off from the rest of the world – sometimes for weeks, sometimes for months, sometimes for years – trying to fill our empty pad of paper or computer screen with words that will illuminate, titillate, amaze and inform the people living in the world."

The creature would tilt her giant green head and stare at you like you were the alien, not her.

"If you close yourself off from the rest of your planet, how do you know if the people living *on* it care about what you write?

"We never really do know," you would say, "because we don't get to ask our readers if they care about what we're writing while we're writing."

The creature would shake her head in dismay. "If you don't get to talk to your readers, then how on earth do you know if your writing is any good?"

"In the end, we don't know if it's any good," you would say. "Most of us doubt the worthiness of every word, every sentence, every paragraph we write. In fact, most of us throw away most of what we write in an attempt to produce what we *want to* write."

The creature's giant green head would start spinning. "And do you ever get to the point in your writing where you do actually write what you *want to* write, where you realize the vision you have for the writing?"

"No, not really," you would say. "The moment you write your first sentence, you know it's not going to be as good as you wanted it to be."

The creature's giant green head would begin to gyrate wildly on her spindly neck covered with orange scales. "So to be a writer," the creature would conclude, "means that you're pretty much condemned to a life of solitude and failure."

"That's right," you would say. "Our life is rather painful."

"Then why does anyone want to be a writer?" the creature would ask.

"Because we can't help ourselves," you would say. "Even though we fail over and over again, we hold out hope that someday someone will read our words and care about what we have to say."

Hope. That's about the only thing we writers have on our side, hope that our readers will care at all about the stories we write. That hope explains why my friend and fellow writer, Mike Mooney, spent almost an entire month holed up in his pain cave – sweating, worrying, his face turning greasy, his eyes turning bloodshot – trying to write something meaningful about writing that other writers might deem worthwhile. He deleted lede after lede, and typed up "thousands of words" that ended up in the trash can.

Despite physical pain in his back, elbows and eyelids, Mike persevered to produce this year's Introduction for Ten Spurs, a meditation on the writing life aptly titled, *The Problem with Writing*. Since Mike wasn't even paid for his painful effort, the green creature from the other planet surely would have asked him why he endured such misery. Only hope, Mike would say, sustained him. "It's hoping you'll send something out into the world that might outlive you," Mike wrote, "and trying not to think about that."

Mike isn't alone. Most writers, even ones who churn out bestsellers that garner effusive praise from critics and adoration from readers, grapple with extreme anxiety and dubiety. "The success of one book doesn't translate into any kind of self confidence in the writing of another," says Khaled Hosseini, who has sold more than 38 million copies of his books, *The Kite Runner* and *A Thousand Splendid Suns*. During a recent publicity tour for his latest mega-book, *And the Mountains Echoed*, Hosseini squelched the illusion that with success the writing gets easier. "Writing is always a struggle," he told Mike Merschel, the book editor of *The Dallas Morning News*. "It's always a journey of self doubt and sort of this ever-present suspicion that you're going to fail. So that's just the inherent part of writing."

Most readers have no idea what their favorite writers go through to produce words that charm them, enthrall them, provoke them, possess them and inspire them to keep reading. "People tend to look at successful writers, writers who are getting their books published and maybe even doing well financially, and think they sit down at their desks every morning feeling like a million dollars," says Anne Lamott, in *Bird by Bird*, a popular book on writing, "…that they take a few deep breaths, push back their sleeves, roll their necks a few times to get all the ricks out and dive in, typing fully formed passages as fast as a court reporter."

But Lamott says that that notion is "just the fantasy of the uninitiated." The hard truth is that for anyone who wants to make a career out of writing, your choices are limited. "You can either type or kill yourself," a writing friend lamented to Lamott.

To overcome the inevitable failures and frustrations of their early morning pecking at the typewriter, some writers, including famous ones, find endless ways to escape from the work at hand. Joyce Carol Oates, for example, literally runs away from her writing. "The structural problems I set for myself in writing, in a long, snarled, frustrating and sometimes despairing morning of work, for instance, I can usually unsnarl by running in the afternoon," she wrote in a *New York Time*'s essay on writing. "On days when I can't run, I don't feel 'myself,' and whoever the 'self' is I feel, I don't like nearly so much as the other. And the writing remains snarled in endless revisions."

Edmund White, a novelist and cultural critic, deals with the despair and struggles of writing by keeping a "beloved" companion with him in his writing cubicle: his favorite music. "Music for me is a companion during the lovely (and why not admit it? the boring) hours of writing," White wrote in a *New York Times* essay on writing. "Music is perfect, sure-footed, whereas I'm struggling to remember a word, frame a description, invent an action. If for me music is the secret sharer, it is a friend who has no needs and encourages me to trust that beauty can be achieved in this life, at least theoretically."

Yet, in truth, most writers aren't at all sure that the time they spend in their pain caves will yield something beautiful – stories that will catapult them into arms of acclaim and financial riches. Most writers know that deep down that's just wishful thinking. They know that there are reviewers out there – many of them frustrated writers working as journalists – who have their butcher knives sharpened, waiting for the next opportunity to slash their writing to shreds. Lamott knows all about that. "The first two notices I got on this tender book I'd written about my dying, now dead father said that my book was a total waste of time, a boring, sentimental, self-indulgent sack of spider puke."

Perhaps the only thing more painful than having a reviewer butcher your work is having a fellow writer trash your "voice," the very soul of the writer out of which springs their creativity, imagination and distinctive style on the page. Yet in some workshops and creative writing programs, both instructors and students don't hesitate to guillotine a writer's voice if they feel it isn't "authentic." Even Norman Mailer, who stood atop a literary summit for more than a half century, producing 40 acclaimed books, two of which won the Pulitzer Prize, saw his voice chopped to liverwurst by another famous writer, Susan Sontag. In her essay collection, *Under the Sign of Saturn*, she lacerated Mailer's voice. "I, for one, have always found that voice too baroque, somehow fabricated. I admire Mailer as a writer, but I didn't really believe in his voice."

Ouch.

You would think stories like this would leave lesser-known writers than Mailer feeling pretty hopeless, feeling like they'd be better off trying to make a living selling daffodils on a street corner someplace. But thank goodness there's still plenty of writers, writers like those whose work appears in this anthology, willing to live in caves long enough to create stories that shed light on the human condition, stories that make us laugh, stories that make us cry, stories that allow us to see or feel or experience the world in a new way, with greater clarity, sensitivity and awareness.

Take Joanna Cattanach's deeply felt essay, for example. What would you say to the father who abandoned you and dropped out of your life? In "Reunited," Joanna found the word "Dad" is the hardest word of all.

Pamela Skjolsvik took a job on the "right" side of the bars in a county jail as a Detention Specialist. Out of that experience emerged her story, "Build It and They Will Come," and a lesson for readers that jail is misery for the keepers and the kept.

Once upon a war in Vietnam, a little girl walking to school or picking berries might encounter drunken soldiers, or even death. In Amanda Griffith's "Child of South Vietnam," you'll learn what Thai Le Nguyen remembers, and you won't be able to forget.

We all know that weddings can be bittersweet for the father of the bride. But in Iris Podolsky's "Red Stilettos," her closely observed tale of courtship and marriage in a Jewish family, we learn that it can be bittersweet for everyone else as well.

Can you imagine walking across a bed of burning embers? In "The Girl Who Walked Across Fire," Moira Muldoon did just that. Along with Moira, we discover it can be either a journey through hell or something quite different. It's all in the mind.

In Penne Lynne Richards' suspenseful "Unveiling Hope," two young girls kidnapped from their mother in Canada plot their escape from their abusive father. But what if the city you're escaping from is a place you've come to love?

In "Where the Wild Things Are," Sierra Mendez explores how a frustrated 7-year-old who can't speak, can't see and is utterly misunderstood by his caretakers, came alive in the presence of "Wild Things" at Esperanza Farms.

For many teen parents, the words "custody," "visitation" and "rights" invite a cold fear that can make for sleepless nights, and futile, frustrating days in court. In "Samuel is Teething," Susan Fisher takes us inside a Dallas courtroom to show how two teenage parents deal with the all-too-common drama.

You wouldn't think that smoking a cigarette on a Paris street could offer insights into the human condition. But Evan Moore's "A Cigarette on the Champs-Élysées" explores some of the rather peculiar moral lessons he learned from his encounters with a murder fugitive and a pickpocket in Paris. One moral lesson we all can take away: Maybe the best way to handle a thief is offer him a cigarette.

All of these pieces, taken together, prove once again that our stories do matter, that they have the power to touch us in the deepest recesses of our being, in ways no other art form can. But what I hadn't considered, until now, was the torture, deprivation and misery these writers endured to create these beautiful stories without having any idea of what our judges would think of them. All they had was what kept Mike Mooney going: hope. The same hope that keeps us all going.

Acknowledgements

Does anyone read these? Who knows? But with the intent of figuring out how to fully recognize and thank all the people involved in the creation of *Ten Spurs* year after year, I spent hours last year reading Acknowledgements by authors I know, admire and respect: Candice Millard, Gay Talese, Hampton Sides, Susan Orlean, Ted Conover, James Swanson, David Grann, Ken Wells, Diane Ackerman, Melissa Fay Greene, Erik Larson, Bob Shacochis, Susan Casey, Ron Powers, Joyce Carol Oates and Kurt Eichenwald.

In reading their Acknowledgements, I can see that most of these authors agonized over their decisions on whom to thank and to what degree to thank them. Out of fear of failing to thank someone they hadn't thought of, they thanked just about everyone: parents, wives, husbands, children, in-laws, bosses, pets, sources, scholars, archivists, librarians, museums, foundations, typists, editors, literary agents, The Library of Congress, God and "dear friends."

I didn't understand why these writers felt obliged to thank their friends – until I read Susan Casey's Acknowledgments for her book, *Devil's Teeth*, a chilling tale about white sharks and the scientists who study them. "Writing a book," Casey wrote," requires asking your friends to go to extraordinary lengths to help you, even as you neglect them."

Now, I wish I hadn't read Susan's Acknowledgements because the list of friends I've asked to go to extraordinary lengths to help me produce *Ten Spurs* – even as I've "neglected them" – is so long it's embarrassing. Among the neglected are our jurists who spend days, sometimes weeks, reading and evaluating hundreds and hundreds of pages of reported narratives and personal essays submitted to the Mayborn contests each year. Then they gather around a Mayborn conference table in Denton, spending all day debating, arguing, scoring and finally selecting the 50 stories that get into our workshops and the 10 "best of the best" that are published in *Ten Spurs* each year.

And what do they get in return for their sacrifice? A free pot of coffee, cookies and Subway sandwiches to keep them going hour after hour, sparring over who they think rises to the level of "best of the best." So it's high time I acknowledge my friends' contributions and beg them to forgive me for neglecting to thank them enough for their role in birthing *Ten Spurs* year after year. This year's jurists, some of America's finest narrative storytellers and editors, include Tim Rogers, Katie Fairbank, Bill Marvel, Dianne Solis, Walton Muyumba, Mike Merschel, Tom Huang, W.K. (Kip) Stratton, Michael J. Mooney, Zac Crain, Nate Blakeslee, Paul Knight, Jim Hornfischer, Jim Donovan and Ron Chrisman.

As they do year after year, this year's workshop leaders will spend many days and nights reading and critiquing our writers' essays, reported narratives and book manuscripts *before* they come to the conference, and then spend all day Friday before the start of the conference giving each writer what they want most: feedback on how to improve their work. So thank you, Susannah Charleson, Doug Swanson, Bill Marvel, Joan Donaldson, Dave Tarrant, Tom Huang and Michael J. Mooney.

I've also neglected to sufficiently thank my friends and fellow writers who spend days, even weeks, writing thoughtful and provocative essays on our craft and our careers – essays that many publishers would be happy to pay good money for – that appear as an Introduction to each new issue of *Ten*

Spurs. Today, I want to acknowledge, thank and, if I could right now, kiss the feet of bestselling writers like Ron Powers, author of *Flags of Our Fathers*, Bob Shacochis, author of *Swimming in the Volcano*, Ken Wells, author of *The Good Pirates*, Sarah Perry, our first Mayborn Fellow who is making her mark as a writer and editor for *Our State* magazine in North Carolina, and Bill Marvel, author of *Islands of the Damned*. Mike Mooney, author of *The Life and Legend of Chris Kyle: American Sniper, Navy SEAL*, spent about a month slaving away in his pain cave over the writing of this year's Introduction for our seventh edition of *Ten Spurs*. Alas, I'm not sure Mike will ever fully recover from the agony he inflicted on himself and his loved ones writing "The Problem with Writing."

Bill's Introduction in last year's issue of *Ten Spurs* ought to be carved in granite and placed on a pedestal at the Poynter Institute. It's a powerful manifesto that lays out the most persuasive argument I've read anywhere on why great storytelling matters – today, tomorrow and forever. Amen to that Bill.

I should acknowledge that each year, Bill Marvel goes above and beyond the call of duty. In addition to writing last year's Introduction to Ten Spurs, Bill wears many different hats around the Mayborn. He's been a presenter, workshop leader, jurist and associate editor of every edition of *Ten Spurs*, including this one. Bill doesn't know it yet, but I'm also going to also ask him to drive to Archer City once again to mentor a new flock of graduate students attending this year's Archer City Writers Workshop – a week-long residency in Larry McMurtry's book town and birthplace of *The Last Picture Show*, *Lonesome Dove* and other masterpieces. If there's another master of the literary nonfiction genre in Texas, it's Bill.

I also want to acknowledge and thank Noah Bunn and Martha Stroud, two of the most gifted artists I've ever worked with. Noah's so indispensable that we wooed him away from his work in the magazine industry and put him back to work on every project the Mayborn has going: a new conference website, *Mayborn* magazine, *Ten Spurs* and myriad other creative initiatives.

And I wouldn't know what we'd do without Martha Stroud. Two years ago, she moved to Tennessee to take a job as an illustrator for a major newspaper chain. But she forgot to tell us she had moved. I spent weeks trying to reach her, without success. As the pub date for *Ten Spurs, Vol. 7* drew closer and closer, panic set in as I began to contemplate the possibility that Martha's illustrations might not grace the pages of *Ten Spurs* for the first time since we launched our award-winning literary journal. But finally, an email arrived in Noah's inbox from Martha assuring us she'd be happy to do our illustrations once again. Thank you, Martha.

So, dear readers, I hope you appreciate, as much as I do, Martha's evocative, hand-drawn illustrations for each piece in *Ten Spurs, Vol. 7*. That Martha was able to create such magnificent artwork against some draconian deadlines while handling her other full-time job tells you why I consider her indispensable. And I owe a special thanks to Jane R. LeBlanc, who copyedited every essay and reported narrative in this issue, saving us from plenty of boo-boos, and to Tasha Tsiaperas, for lassoing our far-flung essays and reported narratives from *Ten Spurs'* writers into the Mayborn corral.

Introduction
by Michael J. Mooney

There's a dog barking in the distance. I can hear the neighborhood kids playing outside, enjoying a temperate summer evening, an anomaly in North Texas. I want to talk to my fiancée. Or go for a walk. Or play with the dog. I'm tempted to check Facebook, Twitter, email, text messages, the scores of four or five different games. There are so many great stories to read. Part of me wants to wade mindlessly through the Internet, to get lost in a labyrinth of Wikipedia pages and YouTube videos, to learn things I know I'll forget by tomorrow. I don't want to write.

I'm greasy and tired and my eyes feel dry from staring at the screen. I've been working on this for too long, sweating, worrying, running sentences over in my head. I've typed up thousands of words I don't like, deleted lede after lede after lede. I've read parts aloud, scribbled different outlines in notebooks, talked it out a few times with a few different people.

But here I am. Still sitting in front of the keyboard, still hoping the draft I've got open will turn into ... *something*. I'm not even sure who might end up reading this. But I want to tell the story the right way, to get across the right points. This is it though. The point is the sitting still, trying to block out the sounds, the world. Trying to focus, to conjure, to sculpt out of the marble of our minds some new thought about the world. It's sweating, it's feeling anxious and curious and joyous and painful—physical pain, in your back and elbows and eyelids. It's hoping you'll send something out into the world that might outlive you—and trying not to think about any of that. It's about the story. It's always about the story.

Maybe a month ago, my good friend George Getschow asked me to write an introduction to this year's *Ten Spurs* anthology, the annual journal published by the Frank W. Mayborn Graduate Institute of Journalism at the University of North Texas, where I went to grad school. George said he wanted me to write about—these are his words—"becoming a literary journalist."

To be honest, that idea makes me uncomfortable. I'm not sure exactly what that means. What, exactly, makes some journalism "literary" and other journalism less so is a matter of personal taste. What I do is tell stories. I try to make them read like the stories I like to read, the ones that captivate me, motivate me. The stories that make me think about life in a different way. So, in lieu of George's request, I can tell the story about how I started in journalism.

It's tricky though, writing about writing. I want it to sound as romantic as I thought it was when I was young—and sometimes it is. Through the stories I've worked on, I've been lucky enough to go to all sorts of interesting places and meet all sorts of interesting people, and I get to work with some of the coolest, most astute editors in the business. But writing can be terrifying, too. There are deadlines, of course. But the real stress comes from the worrying. You don't want to make a mistake, not with someone's story, not with a single word choice. You don't want to miss an opportunity, a chance to poke a hole in the bubble people put themselves in, a chance to touch someone's heart. You don't want to let down an editor. You really don't want to let down a reader.

So as I'm sitting here, I want to write about the summer of 2005, about fifteen or so strangers showing up one at a time at an old hotel in a small Texas town. It was a Sunday in early July, so hot it hurt. This was my first class in grad school, a three-week course about immersion journalism taught by

George, at the Spur Hotel in Archer City—the hometown of Larry McMurtry, the inspiration for much of his work, the place where he decided to plant his massive antiquarian bookstore—about two and a half hours west of Dallas.

I was excited but nervous. I had almost no journalism experience, and I knew nobody in the class—or in the entire industry, really. I wasn't sure exactly what I wanted to do with my life. I knew I wanted to at least try to write stories like the ones I read in *The New York Times Magazine* and *Texas Monthly*, articles that seemed to take some of the classic storytelling elements from fiction and apply them to real-life, true tales I found myself rereading and talking about anytime I got the chance.

The first person I met when I got to the hotel was Brantley Hargrove. He was tall and blond, wearing shades and a Grateful Dead shirt. I remember thinking that his name seemed much more writer-ly than mine, that the name "Brantley Hargrove" just seemed destined to end up on the spine of some epic Western. The group was an interesting mix of people with ages ranging from early 20s to late 50s. There were lifelong journalists, MFA students trying something new and a few photographers who couldn't resist the chance to escape the hassles of life for three weeks. We all checked into the hotel, introduced ourselves and made small talk. A few of us had a couple drinks. The last person to arrive that night was a tall man about my age, wearing cowboy boots and carrying an old IBM electric typewriter. His name was Paul Knight—another writer-ly sounding name, I thought.

On the first morning of the class, George showed up with hundreds of books, examples of this "narrative journalism," this "creative nonfiction" we would be discussing. He stacked them on the tables in the hotel dining room, under a chandelier made of deer antlers. There was Wolfe and Talese and Thompson and Capote and Didion. Krakauer, Orlean, Lewis, Larson, Remnick, Roach. History, memoir, crime, sports, business, writing about writing. Anthologies from newspapers, magazines, writers who've been popping out great stories for decades. This, George explained by way of encouragement, was the kind of writing we would be attempting while we were here. We'd read a lot, deconstruct a bit, practice with some short passages. Then: off we'd go to find stories.

It took a couple of days, some odd questions, some digging at the library, some riding around with ranchers, some hanging out at the only bar in town—but eventually most of the people in the class did find subjects that seemed worthy of deeper inspection. One woman wanted to write about the old jail, with its ledgers full of hand-written history, a hanging station built in 1910, and the jaw bones of a young Indian woman kept in a jar of formaldehyde. Someone else wanted to write about the elaborate grotto just outside of town and the people who drive from hundreds of miles away to pray at the feet of the Virgin Mary statue there. Brantley found an old rancher-historian and a battleground where Texas Rangers had taken on some of the local tribes—events that directly inspired parts of *Lonesome Dove*. Paul found an old roughneck who wore the years of oilfield work from his wrinkled face to his withered hands.

I decided I'd write about what the locals all called "backroading" and the town's mayor, who, every night after the bar closed, would load his pickup with coolers full of ice and beer and just cruise the moonlit backroads with his buddies, listening to country music and talking about life. Night after night, as they'd take off for the backroads as a small caravan, I'd tag along, riding with whomever invited me. We'd fishtail out of the gravel parking lots then roll through the crisp country darkness at 15 miles per hour with the lights off. There was drinking, singing, laughing, even some crying. It was a subculture full of fascinating, (mostly) loveable characters.

I typed up notes every night. I talked about the story a lot—sometimes even with the men I planned to write about. There seemed to be so many possibilities, so many places to start, so many directions I could go. But then it was time to write. And writing is almost never as much fun as reporting.

If you ask George, he's liable to tell you I was a terrible writer before I got to him. In fact, I sometimes joke that before I met George that summer, I was just a young Bolivian boy who spoke no English at all. The truth is: I've wanted to be a writer for as long as I can remember. I didn't mention it much because being a professional writer of any kind seemed unrealistic, like when you hear a kid talk about wanting to be an actor or an astronaut. But even before I could read or write, I would make books with my mother out of construction paper. I was 4 or 5. I'd dictate a story, and she'd record it in her beautiful penmanship, then I'd illustrate each page. Most of the books were about ninjas, pirates or cows. I also wrote short stories in school, and plenty of essays and research papers. (Once in a while, for a modest amount of cash, I may have even helped a fellow student or two with an occasional assignment.) I took creative writing classes in college. (My dual undergrad degree, from the University of Texas, is in English and anthropology.) There's probably not anything I'd want anyone to read now, but my point is: I'd done *some* writing before going to Archer City.

But yes, that first draft—those first couple drafts—of the backroading story were pretty terrible. I wanted to be literary. I wanted to be gritty and sweeping. Mostly the writing was purple and awkward. At one point I had an entire page about a sunrise. Some pretty words—signifying nothing. It wasn't working.

Then George did something I'd never seen. We met to talk about the many spots where my story went wrong, and he rewrote the first few paragraphs. They were the same words—my words—but it was different. It was direct. It was clear, free of gimmicks. It was…just the story.

During the same meeting, George gave me a copy of a Skip Hollandsworth story from *Texas Monthly* called "The Last Ride of Cowboy Bob." It was an incredible account of a mild-mannered woman who robbed banks dressed as a portly bearded man, completely fooling authorities for years. I'd read and admired that magazine for a long time, but suddenly I noticed how fast the prose read, how there was nothing that drew unnecessary attention to the writer, how the story unfolded naturally. The emotion seemed to come from the spaces between the words.

I rewrote my story for a fifth (maybe sixth) time, but this time I tried to step out of the way as much as possible. I tried to focus on the stories of these men, their troubles, their solutions and the new troubles those solutions brought. (As I write this, the irony of writing about myself not writing about myself is not lost on me.) I quoted from Larry McMurtry more than once, because in many ways these men were re-enacting scenes from McMurtry's own fiction—or re-enacting events that inspired that fiction in the first place. (Likely it was a combination of both.) I wanted readers to feel what it was like in that truck, cruising next to the barbed wire fences and meadows, to understand a little bit about the lives that send people to those backroads at night.

The story was published in the first Mayborn literary journal, *Spurs of Inspiration*. The idea and name came from a conversation on the porch on the last night of the Archer City class. The men I'd written about got copies and read the story. Some were upset at first—the mayor got a bit of flack for driving drunk, but probably less than you'd think—but they all wanted to shake my hand, too. They seemed to respect that I, in one man's words, "told it like it is." I still go back there sometimes, and I still see those men. Some have read it so many times they can quote certain passages of the story back to me. That's a strange, complicated feeling. It made me think about life, about lives, about the power stories have.

See, everything we know in life is in the form of a story. Any memory you have, you have it in the context of a story: where you were, what you were doing, who you were with. But a mere story can never be as powerful as a memory. And there is no time where that is more abundantly clear than when you sit down to type it up. When you retire to some sort of cave, and it's just you and your notes and recordings and memories. You want to make something that moves someone as much as you were moved, and you know you never will.

This is the problem I have writing about Archer City. I know I'll never convey that strange alchemy there, with us and the town and the bookstores and the people. With the words, the hopes, the ambition. No matter how hard I try, I can't give you the feeling I have in my chest when I think about that time.

Of course, most of graduate school wasn't like that. Classes were interesting and stimulating, and I like almost everyone I met there, but I noticed quickly the difference between academic classes and what we had in Archer City.

There's a lot of debate over whether journalism, as a craft, can be taught. Right now, in most schools, it's edified the way we do with most liberal arts. There's history, standard practices, the canon. I'd say a lot of that best prepares someone to be a journalism teacher. (As most English degrees best prepare you to teach English.) But journalism can be taught the way music can be taught. You can teach someone chords, you can let them listen and deconstruct the greatest songs of all time, but at the end of the day, someone either has a tune inside of them, or they don't. You can't teach curiosity or creativity, but you can inspire it.

To that end, in Spring 2006, I was going to New York to visit relatives when George arranged for me to visit what his former colleagues referred to as "his old stomping grounds" at *The Wall Street Journal*. In his time at the *Journal*, George was a finalist for the Pulitzer Prize (in 1984), and he was the youngest bureau chief in the paper's history (which, to my knowledge, is still true). I got to tour the offices, to meet several reporters and editors, and to have a few beers with veteran writer Ken Wells in the bar downstairs. (Ken is the author of *Travels with Barley*, an entire book about drinking beer, so it was quite an honor.) He told me stories about his Cajun grandfather, Catfish Wells, the master storyteller.

The next summer, George had a second class in Archer City, and I found a way to go back. So did Paul and Brantley. One of my fellow students that second time in Archer City was a quick-witted, petite blond woman named Tara Nieuwesteeg. Tara is now a book editor, nightlife columnist and my fiancée. She reads just about everything I write—these words being no exception—before I turn it in. (She's awesome.)

That second year, I also got to meet Gay Talese at the Mayborn Literary Nonfiction Conference, which happens right before the Archer City class. I was supposed to be a sort of graduate school liaison, there to escort him around the hotel and help him with anything he needed. He was extremely generous with his time, inviting me to ask him about anything he'd written. We talked about his first collection of stories (which has since been repackaged and renamed), called *The Overreachers*. We talked about why he injected himself into his famous Sinatra story (he said it was the only way he "could make that scene work"), and why he wrote about himself in the third person in his DiMaggio story (same reason). On the Saturday of the conference, I had lunch with him and Skip Hollandsworth. I can still remember sitting there, listening to them talk about writing, about writers they'd always admired and writers they didn't. I remember Talese talking about Hunter S.

Thompson's legendary Kentucky Derby story. Animated, he said something to the effect of, "the only true thing in that story is that there was a horse race."

I'd read in an interview that Talese took notes on cut up pieces of shirt board. At one point, I asked him about it—I wasn't even sure what a "shirt board" was. He smiled and opened the jacket of his tailored suit. He pulled out a stack of five or six oval-shaped pieces of cardboard. He explained that he cut them himself and rounded the edges so they wouldn't show outside the jacket. The top one had a "1" on it, the next one a "2" and so on. On the first card, he had written down a few names he wanted to remember. (Mine was not on the list.) Then he handed me the second card and told me I could keep it if I wanted to. And I did. (I still use it as a bookmark.)

At the same conference, I entered the new writing contest, the same annual contest that produced the 10 stories in this anthology. My story was about a rundown strip club in Fort Worth and the strange characters who inhabited it. Some were crass, some were shrewd, some were surprisingly— disturbingly—sweet. Again, there was the sitting and thinking. The rewriting. The rewriting again. I wanted readers to feel something, even if I wasn't sure what. I wanted them to see what they'd never see otherwise, to go into the margins of society and come out knowing something more about life. I tried to tell their stories through a series of short vignettes. When the story took second place in the reported narrative category, I got a check for $2,000. It felt like so much money—for writing something. I remember holding that check, photographing it. I remember buying drinks for Paul and Brantley that night—and a scotch for Gay Talese. I remember the scent of Tara's hair when she hugged me. I remember thinking that this life, this being a professional writer, might actually be possible.

By 2007, Paul was working at a newspaper in Alabama. Brantley was working at a newspaper in Wyoming. I was working as an enterprise writer at *The Dallas Morning News*, where I got to work with an entire team of incredible journalists and a very understanding editor. I got to write front-page stories about soldiers and Klingon enthusiasts and middle-aged skate boarders and a church of young, fiery Christians with tattoos and Mohawks. Despite our distance though, Paul, Brantley and I would share our stories over email. Sometimes before publication, sometimes after. We'd give honest feedback, what worked and what didn't, even when we weren't sure exactly why. *Have you tried this? Have you read that?* We talked about which stories we'd like to do and which stories and books we were reading. We talked about wanting to write magazine stories, which were mostly longer, with more time to write and report.

In September of that year I took a job at *New Times*, an alt-weekly in Fort Lauderdale. The same week, Paul started a job with the same company, at the alt-weekly in Houston. And a few months later, Brantley got a fellowship at my paper in Florida. He sat at the desk next to mine. Tara got a job at a book publisher in Boca Raton and started writing the nightlife column at *New Times*. We'd all go to the beach and drink beer and talk about stories. Even when Brantley eventually moved to Nashville and Paul moved to Austin, we'd still talk regularly. When one of us had some big accomplishment— when I had a story selected for Best American Crime Reporting, for example—we would all set aside some time in the evening for a conference call. We'd get George on the phone, too, and he'd gush over us with proud, occasionally rambling, toasts.

A few years ago, Tara and I moved back to Dallas, and I joined the staff of *D Magazine*. I also write for *GQ* and for a few national websites dedicated to longform journalism. (Nieman Storyboard, SB Nation, Grantland and BuzzFeed are among a group of sites leading a sort of renaissance of storytelling right now, aided by aggregating sites like Gangrey, Byliner, Longreads and Longform.)

Brantley moved to Dallas, too. He works for the *Dallas Observer*, where he writes incredible stories about the crime and corruption in Texas. Paul is now an assistant editor at *Texas Monthly*.

Recently, George invited all of us to his house. I had just published an eBook with Little, Brown and Company, the same publisher as Malcolm Gladwell, David Foster Wallace, J.D. Salinger, and writer-cum-billionaire J.K. Rowling. Paul had just signed a book deal with Penguin, another giant in the publishing industry. Brantley had just finished a remarkable story about the terrifying murders of two district attorneys in North Texas. And Tara had just agreed to write a regular bar column in *D*.

We got to George's house, on a lake in the suburbs, just as the sun was going down. We drank bourbon and smoked cigars and looked out over the water. We talked about old times, about that first class in Archer City, about trying to soak in an experience and then pour it out onto the page. Last year, Larry McMurtry auctioned off most of his collection and shuttered 75 percent of the store. The Spur Hotel is for sale, and George doesn't know how many more classes he'll have out there. The later it got, the more emotional George got, listing all of our accomplishments, reminding us how proud he was. It wasn't just the alcohol or the beautiful setting. It was that complicated feeling of nostalgia, that sense of accomplishment mixed with a longing for what was. It was the kind of moment you'd want to record, the kind of experience you'd want to share with others. But it doesn't seem possible. I know the story on the page could never match the feelings of the moment.

So here I am, still trying, still typing. The dogs are all quiet now. The neighborhood kids are inside, asleep. Any plans I might have had for the night are long gone. And I'm reminding myself that this is what it's about. It's being exhausted, missing social obligations, skipping meals. I know that, in theory, the process of creation doesn't have to be painful. And it's not always painful. Reporting is the adventure, whether it's sifting through documents or sitting through a trial or hanging out with extraordinary, fascinating people. Then you have to process it. You have to think. You have to worry. You have to change your mind—and change your mind about changing your mind. You have to bleed, then maybe throw it away.

When it works, it's almost like a trance. Other thoughts, other sounds disappear. You think in Story. If the circumstances are right, you produce, like the soil produces vegetables or a chicken produces an egg. You push, you spill. Nothing becomes ... something. Then more. Then more. It's molting. Or birthing. No matter what the emotion is, if it's worth writing about, you feel something. If it's good enough, you feel all sorts of things. You try to record, for yourself, for others, for history. You can only type and delete and type again.

Then you have to stop. You have to put it out there, whether "there" is *GQ* or an alt-weekly or the Mayborn writing contest. And you hope. Hope might be the most important part of writing that nobody talks about. No matter what you write, you're hoping. You hope someone understands. You hope someone feels what you felt, what your subjects felt. You hope you make your friends and loved ones proud. You hope you help, because that's all you can do.

Best of the Best

Ten
Spurs

Reunited: A Father's Love, A Daughter's Choice

by Joanna Cattanach

He is standing alone outside the train station in downtown Dallas, armed with a cell that can't seem to lose my phone number. Barely 5 feet tall, his bean-brown skin is boiled from years of pushing lawn mowers in the Texas sun.

A brisk March breeze cuts through the near empty city streets this Saturday morning, tunneling down Young Street, where he's waiting for a ride. Waiting for me. He's been waiting for years.

Ben Hernandez wants me to visit his home again. He wants pictures of my son, and a relationship.

After 25 years, he wants to be my father again.

***

At 62, he relishes senior discounts. His donated pants are clean but torn along the hem line, the threads dragging along the ground as he walks. I don't know why that bothers me, but it does. He struggles to pay his bills each month and works a series of odd jobs when he can, where he can. Mowing lawns in the mid-cities a few weeks in the summer or helping a friend drive trucks to Laredo. All cash jobs. The only steady employment he has is ringing the bell for the Salvation Army during the Christmas season. A small, brown lump dressed in layers, he stamps his feet on the Walmart pavement to fight off the numbness in his legs. Eight-hour shifts, six days a week outside, in the rain, the wind, sometimes sleet, often causes him to develop chest colds. But he's proud of what he does. "The rich people in Southlake need me," he says. "They expect to see me each year." He's not supposed to say more than Merry Christmas or God Bless to the shoppers, but each week he sets aside money for peppermint candies and hands them out to children who pass by his red kettle. "I like to see them smile," he says. The Salvation Army usually gives him a ham as a Christmas bonus.

Friends take advantage of Ben, often asking him for money he doesn't have—*Ben, can I borrow $40? I'll pay you next week*. Or favors—*Ben, can you get me some lunch? I can't drive myself*. Always he gives and is frustrated when no one pays him back or they steal from him. "I got me a lawyer," he told me once. "He's a civil lawyer." Some lady jipped him out of $39; he only had $27 in his bank account. The lawyer helped him get the money back and got his bank to waive the overdraft fees.

I wish he'd tell people no. I wish he were upright and regal and an ass kicker. I wish he wasn't so poor. I wish I didn't feel ashamed of him.

Ben is diabetic but eats pan-fried food and drinks sweet tea. The son of a migrant worker, he speaks with a slow, thick Texan accent. Too thick for a Mexican man. "Hell-o," he says on the phone, hill-country like. "Did ya' get your ol' check yet?" But he knows his mother's language. Cruz was her last name, I think. Her people are from somewhere in south Mexico. He knows a good recipe for enchiladas and the best place for huevos rancheros on Fort Worth's North Side. When I hear him speak the language I can't remember, the words I struggle for, the verbs I can't conjugate, he is transformed. He is my legacy. His brown skin, those black-brown eyes—my eyes—are reminders of my heritage, and I belong, finally.

It's like this for adopted children like me. No matter how long the time or how much you've accomplished, there are always strands of memory that prevent you from being someone else's child. Case workers, judges and my adopted parents created a new childhood for me. My name was changed. You're not Hernandez anymore; you're Cattanach. I got a new grandma. I got a haircut. And though I branched out, I grew, I began to thrive in new earth, with new parents and sunshine in a house without roaches, in air without cigarette smoke, I never really felt rooted. They didn't do anything wrong. My new family didn't love me less. I did blossom like a cactus plant in a rose garden, but no amount of love or grooming could make me a rose.

I've read stories about children reunited with birth parents after adoption. Often you'll see some mother squeezing tears into a hanky, talking about how she was young, she was scared and she always wondered what happened to her son or daughter. There are investigators who specialize in finding adopted children and reuniting them with their birth parents. Some do it for free. Others charge a fee. There are also websites that help adopted children find their birth parents. Television cameras love this sort of thing. The lens focuses in on that coveted, made-for-TV moment when a parent and child reunite. They might cry, stare into each other's eyes and whisper words of longed-for relief: "I've waited for this moment," the mother might cry out. "I've missed you," the daughter might reply.

My reality is far different, far more complex, far more painful.

As reunions go, ours has not been especially heartwarming. There aren't hugs and kisses or hours-long conversations. Instead there is awkwardness and long stretches of silence and missed phone calls.

Even for those reunited with tears of joy, there are layers of grief and anger and hurt that simply cannot be ignored. What no birth parent wants to admit and every child of adoption knows is this: There was a good reason a child was placed in adoption. Often it is because the birth parent was not capable, still isn't capable of being a good parent. Poverty and mental illness prevented my birth parents from caring for me.

But Ben and I never talk about those missing 25 years he wasn't in my life, nor the circumstances that forced my younger brother and me into foster care. All I know is that we were two of the 5,400 children placed in foster care by the State of Texas in 1982 and two of the 700 children adopted in 1984.

Like us, children in foster care today will remain in the system on average over two years. Though we were adopted, we shared a three bedroom trailer with—at times—up to five foster kids, including me. Some of my "brothers" and "sisters" had scars from their moms and dads—burns from a boiling pot of water left on a hot stove within reach of a toddler's curious fingers. Some kids were violent and mean—and I was only 3. Others screamed and kicked and had to be dragged out of the house when the social worker came to get them for a home visit.

Most of them were eventually adopted, but today, many children in foster care —almost 10 percent, nationally—age out of the system at 18 having never been adopted. Thankfully, we were not among them. My brother and I were adopted by our first foster family and not separated from each other as are so many siblings.

But like so many children before me, and those still to come, forgetting is hard, and Ben Hernandez hasn't been a welcome addition in my life.

As any child of adoption will tell you, inevitably there will come a time when you wonder why you don't look like your new mom and dad. You will feel the sting in family portraits as your brown curls and chocolate *ojos*, and round Mexican-ness stick out in the framed photo of you alongside blonde-haired and blue-eyed Anglos. It's in the eyes of strangers: "How come you don't look like your sister?" And even the smallest bits of information blood-kids take for granted: How much did I weigh at birth? What were my first words? Did my mom hate mushrooms as much as I do? No matter how great your adopted life is, how wonderful your new mommy treats you, it is impossible to forget who you come from and harder still not to wonder about your past.

And I am no different.

***

After weeks of missed phone calls and near-daily voice messages—I had 100 waiting voice mails from Ben—I couldn't avoid him any longer.

 It's like this for us: Him pushing and grasping and seeking. Me retreating and hiding and fleeing. He keeps asking for my new address, but I'm afraid he'll show up at my house one day unannounced, so I've lied for the last year always promising, next week, next month, soon I'll mail him a letter.

I have no intention of doing so. Not yet. Maybe never, especially not after what happened last year. He sent a Dallas police officer to my home on a welfare call to see if I was still alive. I didn't return his phone calls for a month, and he thought I might be dead.

I finally answered the phone a few days later.

"Joanna?" he asked. "It's your dad, Ben." He always identifies himself as *my* dad. I don't like it. I don't consider myself *his* daughter.

"Yes," I replied, trying not to sound as frustrated as I feel. I hate when he calls, which is all the time and any time of day. Sunday mornings at 7 a.m. or 1:30 p.m. or whenever he thinks I'll answer, multiple times a day for weeks until I answer the phone. And though I try to calm myself, I feel tension stiffen my shoulders and roll through my body, each muscle tightening in response to a simple phone call. I can't breathe sometimes.

"Hey, I got a blanket for the baby. Can I give it to you? Are you doing something this weekend? Can I see you?" He rattles out the same speech each time. Always he has something to give me. Five dollars for my 28th birthday. A ring he ordered from a catalogue. "It's almost here. Do you know what size ring you wear, because I ordered a seven and a half," he asks over the phone. Or something to show me. His birth certificate one time. "Look, it says here I was born in Wy-oming. I'd sure like to go back there." And his letters express the same sentiment written in large, childish script, three to four sentences that take up half a page—HOW ARE YOU?

As usual I hedge at his latest request. "I'm not sure if I'm doing anything Saturday," I say.

Does he ever consider what I want? Or think about how painful it is for me to have him back in my life? Does he think about how much he hurt me all the years he didn't call or buy me rings from a catalogue? Does he know how foolish I felt growing up hoping to find a birthday card from him in the mail only to be disappointed?

So many foster care and adopted children dream of this kind of opportunity, but not me. And yet it found me just two weeks before my wedding, in 2008, when a blood cousin I'd never met left me a voice mail.

"Your father called," stranger cousin said. "Your mother is in the hospital dying."

I thought it was a joke. The only father I knew died of cancer the year before. And I'd sure as hell know if my mother were in the hospital, let alone dying.

And just like that, without warning, at the happiest moment of my life, *he* came back in. What happened next is a blur. I called my adopted mother. She was shocked. We all were. No one had heard from my mother, Verna, in years. Her mental illness had scared away whatever family she had left. And my adopted mother assumed Ben was dead. "I thought he committed suicide," she said.

I went to the nursing home to see what was left of my schizophrenic mother the same day I got the phone call, so I suppose in some way I did bring this on myself. I could have not gone. I could have deleted the voice mail.

Maybe it was because she was dying. Maybe I needed closure. Maybe I bought into the reunited-and-it-feels-so-good mentality. What I found was a screaming mess off her meds. Verna didn't know who I was and didn't care. She wanted cigarettes and a cola. The bloated pear-shaped figure in a wheelchair smelled of pee and creamed corn. She begged me, her forgotten daughter, to take her home. *I want to go home!* She went home just two months later, alone in her bed and later in a pauper's box, cremated cut-rate by the Greenwood Funeral Home in Fort Worth. She died from heart failure and complications brought on by diabetes.

But my story isn't about Verna. It's about Ben. It always has been. About the father who knew me before I was born. Ben, whose tenderness makes hating him so hard. Ben, who hasn't stopped calling me. I don't know why I gave him my phone number. Maybe it was because he looked so small, so diminished standing outside of the nursing home that day in 2008.

I thought at first the man pacing out front was homeless. He shuffled along the pavement carrying a backpack. And then, though I hadn't seen him in two decades, I knew he was my father. I still carried that childhood dream that he'd be *somebody*. A veteran, a war hero, someone who was messed up for a good reason. Deep down, like all children, I wanted to be proud of my father. Instead, a warm tide of embarrassment washed over me as I realized the vagabond pacing outside the nursing home was my dad. Why did he have to look so poor? Why couldn't he smell clean? And smile with a full set of teeth?

When I was a teenager, I fantasized about my birth parents. Confused and searching for identity, I was one of the lucky ones who had photos—seven to be exact—of me before adoption. Me in a car. Me in Verna's lap. Me holding Ben's hand. All chosen to seem normal, but I knew there wasn't anything normal about our home life. There were no "Mommy's Favorite" t-shirt shots or "Daddy's Little Girl" poses. There were no bows in my hair or shiny black Mary Janes or white ankle socks with lace. Where was my first Christmas? My first tooth? My naked-in-the-bathtub photo? All I have are seven celluloid copies of a little girl with big brown eyes taken by surprise from an un-focused distance.

And then there was the long, gray silence after a welfare worker took my brother and me and left us with strangers. I could hear the new world around me. I could smell fried eggs and pancakes. I could touch the baby dolls. But I couldn't function, and so I slept on the bunk bed in the shared bedroom with my new "sisters," in the strange house with the toys I could play with—*Don't you want to play?*— and was told when to get up, when to pee, to brush my teeth like a good little girl, only to shut my eyes and fall back to sleep in the comforting silence, in the choked tears of a toddler who finally realized mommy and daddy weren't coming to get her.

I did emerge from sleep, but when the other foster kids would get loud, I'd crawl into a closet, over piles of shoes and hide behind my foster mom's house coats and church skirts. The thin cotton covered my face in the dark, cool silence. I could hear my foster parents call for me, I could see them through the gap in the closet door, but I refused to answer them. I hoped they'd never find me. But they always did. *What are you doing hiding in there, silly girl?* They took away my bottle. They had rules and consequences. We had to clean our plates. For hours I'd sit at the kitchen table mute and angry in front of a bowl of goulash or split pea soup. But I learned to eat it—I had to. I spoke again. I got used to seeing new kids, troubled kids, hurt kids, come and go. When my foster parents finally adopted my brother and me, I got used to that, too.

I learned early on adoption is about adaptation. And a kid who escapes the foster wheel learns to adapt quickly. You *can* learn to call a stranger mommy. It's hard at first. You may just wait to catch her eye—*Can I have more milk?* Or tug at the back of her dress—*Um, I need to go potty.* But eventually you can say it. New mommies want to hear it. It's not so bad...eventually.

I hadn't come from home situations like my foster brothers and sisters. No one beat the crap out of me or threw me against a wall. There weren't drugs in our house. Ben and Verna did love my brother and me. And our foster home was one of the better ones. Our foster, now adoptive, parents gave us a real childhood, with real memories. My foster mother bought me a powder blue Easter dress with a big bow on the butt and fluffy 1980s sleeves. I wore it every week to church with white lacey socks and black Mary Janes. I felt beautiful in that dress. My sister—my adopted parents' only biological child—treated me like her pet puppy, and I waggingly played along. Ten years older, she had me memorize the lyrics to '80s pop songs. We'd sing Cyndi Lauper tunes in her Yugo on the way back from the grocery store. Those were happy times.

But I thought often about my real mom and dad—Are they going to come get me? Will they send me a birthday card? Do they think about me? And later, when I was older, when I got tired of waiting and tired of feeling different—I hate them!

***

I tell myself each time Ben calls that I won't answer. My adopted mother warned me to be careful. "He may want something from you." At each awkward meeting, I keep waiting for the other shoe to drop. Will he ask for money? A place to stay? He did once borrow $20. And as I handed it to him, I felt a secret vengeance. I knew it! I knew he was a phony. A few weeks later, he paid me back in full.

But there have been other moments like the time he disappeared for a month. I'd gotten so used to ignoring his phone calls that when he stopped calling, I grew concerned. I'd visited his home before; I stayed for five minutes, perched on a smelly futon afraid to touch anything. Ben's Social Security check affords him an illegal sublet in a crime-ridden area of Fort Worth. He's an easy target.

Finally, his brother called me. He hadn't seen Ben in weeks. His phone was cut off. I checked the

Tarrant County morgue's website for John Does. I read autopsy reports hoping that the "male, Hispanic, 5 feet tall" was not my father but also secretly wanting an end to our strained relationship.

Ben showed up a month later. He had gone to Oklahoma but didn't tell anyone.

This is what reunion is about. You inviting the crazy back in. You having to be involved when you don't want to and feeling guilty for not caring more. Why do I do this to myself? I can stop all of this. I can change my phone number. I can burn his letters. I *can* forget Ben. I have before.

I've given myself permission to let go, but he won't.

You see, Ben never let go. He was just gone.

I live in Dallas now and never knew Ben and Verna lived in Fort Worth all the years I was separated from them. Just like I never knew my Aunt G forwarded the letters I wrote her to Ben's family. My adopted mother made sure we wrote and visited our great Aunt G, Verna's aunt, until Aunt G died in 1999. I wrote Aunt G about school, about my new life, my dreams and desires. My adopted mother sent her our school photos. The state does allow for continued contact after adoption—though most families opt not to.

I never inquired about Ben in my letters. I never wanted to know about him. I'd always assumed he was the reason I was taken. Because I couldn't remember him, I blamed him. But he memorized those letters. I know, because he asked me once if I still wanted to be a doctor. I'd played around with the idea when I was in high school before I enrolled in freshman chemistry in college and figured out math and science and blood were not for me. There is no way he would have known that without reading my letters.

The beaten man with missing teeth and giveaway clothes is the polar opposite of me. He is the product of 25 years without his children. He is a shadow of the moments he should have had. His absence has deprived him of the joy a father gains through parenthood.

I have what he was never able to keep. I've taken hundreds of photos of my son in the bath tub, wiggling on the changing table, asleep, awake, crying, angry in an Easter bunny outfit he does not want to wear. My little boy wears Baby Gap and giggles when I make faces at him—*peekaboo!* His father and I argue about where he will go to college. We spend weekends at the park together and take turns at night rocking our son back to sleep—*rest, baby boy, just shut your eyes and rest.* We're buying our first house, someplace with a yard, in a safe neighborhood with great schools.

Though I've allowed myself these brief moments of time with Ben, this has not been easy for my family. My husband has difficulty with the situation. He doesn't know how to address Ben and feels as frustrated as I do when Ben tries to act like my father. I do not call him Dad; I call him Ben. And though I have a blood brother—Ben's namesake in fact—he refuses to share any kind of a relationship with our found father. It's just too hard and too strange for him. My younger brother was a baby when we were in foster care. He attached himself to our adopted family and doesn't want to look back. I understand completely.

So when our father asks, "How's Benji?" I'm honest but not hopeful. He's always good. He's always fine. And nothing more. Ever.

I've learned to set boundaries. I have to do this for my own emotional health. I have to protect my son and myself because deep down I still wonder if Ben is going to disappear again and how bad it will hurt when he does. Yes, Ben has met his grandson. I couldn't deny him. And though my little boy is a mere 5 months old, I want him to know that he wasn't born rootless like I've felt for so long. My baby comes from people.

I don't know why I feel the need to protect myself from this man. Maybe when you can't quite size up your enemy, you have to build strong defenses. Maybe it's because he never talks about the missing years. He never mentions our adoption but always inquires about my adopted mother. "How is Mrs. Cattanach?" I'm 31 years old, and he still sends me little girl birthday cards. But he also offers me small glimpses of myself. "You used to love tomatoes as a little girl," he said once. "You never sat down at the kitchen table, always running around making noise," he said, smiling. He gifts me memories. I know it's selfish, but I like having someone in my life who still treats me like his little girl.

I want to see him as a nice man, not a failure of a father.

For now, I can decide how much Ben I want and when and for how long. And I derive perverse pleasure from that at times. And finally, control.

For his part, Ben has told everyone about me. He always introduces me as his daughter—*es mi hija*—to strangers, to the disheveled homeless in downtown Fort Worth he hangs out with sometimes. Slowly, I've met other family members as well. I have an Uncle Frank and an Uncle John, Ben's half-brothers. They've welcomed me back into the family. They remember me as a little girl. They have families and successful lives and good health and have thrived, like I have, in the ways Ben has not.

But where do I go from here? How far do I let this little trip down memory lane take me? I worry about what will happen if his health starts to fail. I'm not prepared or willing to become a primary caregiver. It's all too much at times, and yet not enough. Despite my own reservations about our awkward relationship, I've requested my case file from the Texas Department of Health and Human Services, the state agency that handles foster care and adoption cases. I need to know what happened. I need to see the truth through a social worker's notes, not Ben's wishful thinking or seven lousy snapshots. Some two years after my request I'm still waiting. I guess the state isn't any more interested in mailing me my past than I am receiving it.

***

I pull up to the curb and spot Ben sitting on a bench outside the train station. He walks over to the car—left foot, right foot—not really walking straight but wobbling, teetering from toe to toe. Not drunk. Diabetes has cut off some of the circulation in his lower legs, and he can't move as fast anymore.

He's got a friend with him this time. "Hey, this is my friend, Juan Cantu." Ben leans into the passenger side door and throws his backpack on the floor board.

Oh, God! Will I have to give him a ride? My baby is in the back seat.

But Juan is waiting for another bus, "*Mucho gusto,*" Juan says and tells Ben they'll meet up later to take the train back to Fort Worth.

"That's my friend Juan," Ben says. "He's 78 years old and likes to get out." Ben has lots of friends. Old friends, disabled friends, shady friends, church friends. He's like that.

He buckles his seat belt and I pull away from the curb. We drive to the restaurant in silence. I want to embrace this more. I don't want to be ashamed of Ben, but I just don't know how. He makes hating him so hard.

In the four years we've reconnected, I've never once called him Dad. I just can't. I can't hug him. It hurts too much. I spent years calling someone else dad and accepting a parental relationship that too often felt one-sided. I couldn't be a Cattanach fully, not really. And I couldn't be the round-face girl with *pecas*, freckles, either.

The waitress points us to a table, and Ben immediately orders the senior special. My son Gabriel is getting antsy in his car seat. Like most babies, he hates being confined when he can be carried. I unbuckle his straps and set him on my lap. He looks at Ben and smiles. Babies are like that.

Long strands of drool pour out of his gummy mouth—*goo*, he coos.

Ben watches Gabriel, "He'll be talking soon." He hands me $30, "for the baby," he says. I noticed dirt under his fingernails.

The waitress arrives with our breakfast dishes, and Ben announces over scrambled eggs and white toast, "You know, my father isn't buried far from here." He's always doing that. He's always shooting one over my wall. I live in Dallas, and my grandfather is buried here. I never knew that!

We're quite a pair. Me in an Ann Taylor top and designer jeans, grasping a chubby baby boy who's intent on sticking his fingers in my omelet, and Ben in paint-spattered dress pants and a white *guayabera*, a Mexican wedding shirt. Ben has gained some weight. "I moved in with my stepdad in Saginaw," he says. "He needs help getting around, so I make him lunch during the day."

The baby is wiggling on my lap and makes lovey eyes at the couple seated behind us.

"Do you want to hold him?" I ask Ben and almost immediately regret it.

"Yes," he says and reaches forward for his grandson, his first grandchild, his only grandchild. Gabriel immediately starts to cry. "I knew he'd do that," Ben says laughing, bouncing the baby on his lap. "He just can't stand to be away from Mama."

Ben takes off his glasses and makes silly faces at Gabriel who laughs and shakes his thick baby arms. I can smell Ben's cologne from across the table. He got cleaned up for me.

This is the only way he knows how to be a father. He is never going to be rich or powerful. He's not my hero. He's my father, and I am his daughter. This is going to be hard, this future we have and this past we share and these genes that connect us.

So how do we move forward?

I reach for the baby and cradle my crying son who's back to happy again and look over at Ben who's beaming with a new-found pride. The shoulders I can't embrace are shaking with laughter, and there in Ben's big brown eyes, my eyes, my son's eyes is the answer—hope.

"Don't worry," Ben says. "He'll get used to his grandpa."

Samuel is Teething

by Susan Fisher

Editor's Note: The names in this piece have been changed because the subjects were minors at the time of the court hearing. Shauna, now 18, is still living with her parents.

Samuel is teething. His gums are swollen with the wait, alternating between itching and aching for weeks. Mercifully, he's asleep.

Shauna Garcia, his young mother, shifts the drowsy toddler from her left side to her right, trying her best not to wake the boy as she reaches for her purse on the floor beneath the courtroom's wooden bench. He isn't hungry, she knows that, but when his gums start bothering him, she's learned a bottle is the best remedy to help everyone around them maintain their sanity.

Shauna and Samuel have been sitting in a child support hearing now for over three hours. Shauna was told that the weeks she'd spent arguing with Samuel's father, Tony Sona, about an agreed order for child support and paternity would be "in everybody's best interest." And today—proud she'd finally talked him into attending the hearing—would be her reward: some certainty her son would be acknowledged and cared for.

Endless case numbers are droned in a rhythm not unlike that of the sluggish ceiling fan overhead, a duet of dullness and heat. Under the whirring fan, every day of every week of every year, parade young parents, mostly mothers, asking the court to enforce DNA test results and declare "baby daddies around the state.

If any one of these parents were a bank, their outfits would be different, but so would their outcomes. Credit card deadbeats, hot check writers and the like rarely get away with the kind of institutional robbery supported in this room. Yet getting courts in Texas and other states to enforce child support laws is often too expensive for parents to pursue.

Shauna won't set Samuel down, hoping his dormant amnesty will continue. Every time she shifts him from one arm to the other, she trades numbness for an ache in the empty arm, and she's afraid the Bailiff might hear her moans. The alternative to this clumsy two-arm ballet is even worse. If Samuel were to wake up and see Shauna, in all her misery, he'd let loose with a wail so disturbing it had once driven her from a Walmart before he'd taken his second breath.

And if Samuel started wailing now, in this warm, stale room, she was not only afraid he wouldn't stop, but that she might join him. She'd been waiting, too: for his father before she realized he wouldn't be coming around much anymore, for her pregnancy to end, to heal from the birth, and finally to be sure that she could keep her son safe from the moody restlessness of his father and the chaos of his own family.

Shared parenting was a daydream: parenting for Shauna had begun the moment she read her pregnancy test, taken a shower, and secured a job before suppertime. Samuel's father was parenting only in fits and starts. And when the issue of child support came up, it was mostly fits.

Samuel has lots of drowsy, teething peers around the State of Texas, more than most other states. And most of these young parents are bound in the same tense, unhappy struggles. They're often made to feel that they have shamed their parents, their congregations, their relatives, their schools. The "shame" is magnified for young mothers for the simple reason that their parenthood shows. If they remain in school, they're often segregated from their peers. And out of fear of their family's reaction, many young mothers don't acknowledge their pregnancy and postpone the prenatal care their baby needs. The one thing most of these young mothers can't seem to avoid, however, is ending up, sooner or later, in a room like this one. While no longer the growth sector it had been in the 90s, today's teenage parents face a much more hostile economic climate.

In the absence of information and birth control, the result is youngsters trying on responsibilities like fashion trends: custody agreements, child support orders, budgets, their own parents ("I mean like, how can they ground me? I've already got to be here for the night feedings...").

Texas is no exception. Like other state governments around the country, family services, educational programs and medical care for children have all been slashed. By the time the children born to these children are around 3, most of their teen fathers will be in arrears on their child support payments, turning young fathers into criminals. And instead of spending toddler birthdays at Chuck E. Cheese's, these couples frequently spend their child's "special day" in the very unsentimental child support courtrooms of Texas.

The judge calls another name that isn't hers. Shauna's tense, weary gaze meets Samuel's father seated across the aisle, his hands fidgeting in his lap. That gaze, like so many lately, contains no emotion; certainly no furtive, supportive signal that surely the next name called would be his, or hers or the baby's. No recognition beyond that of a man unsure what to do with his hands, or of a woman who has none free.

More than gazes were exchanged, of course, between these two during their senior year when they met, courted and conceived. Shortly after sharing the news with Tony that they would be parents, Shauna learned a lesson about which she'd heard plenty from the aunts who'd gather for card games around her mother's table: he'd taken up with a younger woman, a junior who'd caught his fancy and whose figure wouldn't be changing.

Even though he had a "new woman," he promised Shauna that he would be responsible for her and his son. The same day she learned she was going to have a baby, she got a part time job. But as she looked at her expanding waistline and the constricting balance on her bank statement, she knew she would have to do more. Her parents weren't happy, but she hadn't suffered at their hands like one or two others in her class had. She could stay with them as long as she needed to, and they agreed to make her next step possible: within six weeks of giving birth, Shauna attended her first weekend with the Army Reserve, a way to ensure she could manage college tuition and keep her son insured, too.

Yet money wasn't the most challenging part of this new adventure. For many teen parents, the words "custody," "visitation" and "rights" invite a cold fear that can make for sleepless nights. Tony's visits were rarely announced any further in advance than on the gravel at the head of her driveway. And these short, erratic visits were generally more work than help. Often he'd slam the door of his shiny new truck and shuffle toward her parents' doorway. Shauna would try to head him off, afraid of what her father might say or do if he witnessed these unannounced visits.

Sometimes Tony would hand her an oil-smudged, multi-creased envelope with cash, never more than $50. Other times he would bring "gifts" to "my boy," surprises like a *queso*-stained, size medium Cowboy's jersey; a Phillips screwdriver; or a new lure with a bright blue feather. "You know how to make this safe, right? You just put a cork on the end..." Tony handed the bright blue, feathered hook to Shauna. He saw the look on her face, even in the dark: "Hell, Shauna, nothing's safe enough, is it? If that's how you feel, just tell him the second-best bet is a freshly squashed frog." He climbed back into the cab and spun gravel again, staring in the rear view mirror to see if she laughed when he wasn't looking.

It was after that visit that Shauna knew she had to do something "legal" about this. Something that might cost money, would surely cost time and would probably not be pleasant. But it would be more pleasant, she thought, than the night Tony showed up with paper that said he had the legal right to drive out of her driveway with Samuel. The sound of gravel as the pickup truck spun out of that driveway was the sound that echoed over and over in Shauna's mind, fueling her double shifts and finally the night off she asked for to get ready to go to court.

***

While other wait staff freshened their lipstick after shifts, Shauna was calling home to see if her mother needed her to bring home anything from the store. It had been nearly a year since she got to leave with her cohorts. But that night she had a special date. She'd asked her boss to leave early so she could take three buses to a downtown family law clinic where single parents can get free advice and forms for child support, custody and modifications.

Shauna is gorgeous. She smiled as men stared at her on the bus. She knew a romance could happen any time. But not now. Not until she had the paternity and child support paperwork she needed that have Tony's name signed under the word "AGREED."

Nothing will make a young woman appear more mature, more ready to parent, than to get that other parent to agree to the orders. The court will almost always sign child support papers when two parties work out issues together before they appear in court. The clinic had told her that on the phone, the clinic where she was now headed, the clinic where they'd show her how to put together her custody papers.

The clinic was packed. Perhaps 40 women (and one man) sat at a double-long, wooden table in the middle of the room. The top of this table was covered with crawling, pawing, laughing, wobbly children. The older, sophisticated 9- and 10-year-olds rolled their eyes.

Every parent inside the room was juggling with five pieces of paper per child. Pencils and a few pieces of paperwork were grabbed from drooling mouths, removing first pages, portions of signatures. Amidst the mayhem, Shauna sat down and finished her questionnaire, waited to speak with an attorney, waited for a second set of papers;, filled those out and waited for a coordinator to give her a date.

Two hours after she'd walked in, Shauna had her paperwork that said, in legal language, there would be NO impulse midnight fishing trips, NO showing Samuel off at Tony's watering hole, NO to the 12-year-old car seat Tony had purchased, NO to the slurring father taking his son in that car seat to the bar where they sold the lures and NO to the unscheduled spitting gravel at the end of her driveway. On her ride home that night, Shauna tried to clutch the papers without wrinkling them. One word was in all caps: AGREED. It was dark on the bus. So Shauna used her cell phone's light to read it over and over again.

***

That was a different time of day, and a different month. It had been cool on the bus that night. Now the air in the courtroom was stuffy, sultry, as if it contained everyone's anxiety-induced perspiration. Older siblings crawled across the benches. Babies woke up, protested, then fell back into a fitful sleep. Mothers withstood the bailiff's glare and changed diapers on the court's benches. Earlier, the bailiff had announced that the air conditioner was in fact on, but by this time it was a matter of faith, not relief.

When the couple at the bench finally finished up with the judge, Shauna took advantage of a brief recess to finish her search for Samuel's bottle, just in case. She refused to leave the courtroom. She had waited, waited, waited, and she wouldn't risk missing her name when it was called. Or Tony's name. Or Samuel's name. She would use the restroom later, after she got the paper, the paper with the signatures that would make it easier for her to sleep tonight. Tony changed his mind about everything, almost by the week, and she wanted those signatures because she needed a rest from his moods worse than she needed to use the restroom. She wanted ink, good and dry, and then he couldn't change his mind about anything.

The judge called another name that wasn't theirs. Shauna remembered her last argument with Tony. Back from the clinic and surprised by a midnight visit, she'd shown him the applications she'd filled out. But when he tried to read the papers, she realized it wasn't the darkness that was making him squint. "We'll just see about this," was all he said. But this time the gravel made a slow, soft crunch as Tony hesitated at the end of the driveway before he drove away.

Arriving at the courtroom, she was relieved when she spotted him sitting inside. After all the phone calls and bus rides and hassle, waiting inside the courtroom for her name to be called didn't bother her at all. She remembered that he'd called her once after that night, and that was when she realized for the first time that Tony was scared. She would have felt some relief, or pity, or even some companionship for her own fears if she hadn't listened as carefully as she had.

It was clear that Tony was scared a judge might make him pay more child support than he could afford. He'd bought his new truck to celebrate his "new woman's" pregnancy, had driven it to his parents' home to show them all on the Saturday he'd signed for it. Tony's pregnant girlfriend had come out of the house first, and seemed happy that Tony was happy showing off his shiny new machine.. And his parents had surprised him, as well—this truck wouldn't have been possible, he knew, if his parents hadn't invited his new family to join his old one. His parents were already hosting his older brother's small family, an uncle from South Texas who was looking for a job and their aging grandmother. There was just enough room, one last small bedroom, which Tony thought would be perfect for his family of three. And a great spot in the driveway for the truck.

Shauna knew how he felt about that vehicle, knew he'd celebrated the news he'd be a father by his new girlfriend by buying rims that cost $1,200. Times four. On a few occasions, Shauna had taken a ride with Tony so he could show the baby off to his friends. He held Samuel up in the air and showed him more like a fancy hood ornament than his newborn. Sometimes he'd drive them to houses where his friends walked around the truck a couple times before they'd peek in the window at Samuel.

Shauna figured taking Tony to court would end her troubles and increase his. She was trying her best to be reasonable. She'd agree to the state-mandated minimum level of child support so Tony wouldn't have to sell his new subwoofers. But Tony didn't want to even pay the minimum amount. He told her no judge could make him pay her money because he was already starting a new family. Shauna didn't argue with him. She simply explained that if he came to court and signed the paperwork titled "Agreed," that the judge would let them do things pretty much the way they wanted. He asked if that meant he could keep his rims and his subwoofer. She said she would agree to that.

Her strategy seemed to work. He is sitting in the courtroom across from her. And despite the long, hot wait, he hasn't left yet. If he was going to bolt, she figures, he'd have done it two hours ago.

Another couple approaches the judge. Because the front row is now empty, Shauna can now see and hear through the sounds of babies crying and the undulating heat that moved the fan around. "Your Honor, I can't keep coming back. This is the third time we've been here, and he had some story for you, and this time my boss said I can't keep taking these half days off..." Shauna looks at the young man standing in front of the judge. He's wearing a plaid shirt and jeans, even though the sign in the hall had established a "no jeans" policy. She can see that he is going to win and that the woman is going to lose. "Judge, there's just nothing I can do, you see that, don't you? When somebody steals every single one of your tools out of the back of your truck..."

Now the woman's shoulders are moving, though Shauna can hear nothing at all. She can only feel dread creeping up her arm. The judge sets a continuance; the man in the plaid shirt shakes his head, tells the judge he'll "do his best" until the next time and saunters out of the room. The woman stands, fixed. The court reporter leans over and hands her tissue; as she turns to walk out of the courtroom, she is crying and shaking her head. "I can't come back again," she murmurs.

"GARCIA, SHAUNA, AGREED PATERNITY AND CHILD SUPPORT..."

Shauna jumps. Her eyes dart toward Tony. He turns rigid, except for his fingers, which are still fidgeting.

"AGREED?" The judge seems to be asking a question. Shauna shifts the still miraculously sleeping Samuel, partially stands and answers "Yes, Your Honor..."

"Sit down m'am, it's not you I want to talk to." Suddenly, Shauna feels like she is a child in trouble, unsure what she's done wrong.

"AGREED?" the judge repeats, seeming to ask the entire court. "Mr. Sona, are you present in the courtroom?"

Tony jumps to his feet. "Here, Your Honor".

The judge stares at Tony. "Mr. Sona, come up here, son." Tony ambles up the aisle, alternately muttering, "excuse me" as he steps on several feet along the way to the bench.

"Now what kind of nonsense is this from a schoolboy?" the judge says. "You think you know everything, don't you? You don't. You are very, very young to be making this kind of decision. Do me a favor: turn around and look at the men in this courtroom. Just look. Now do you think there are a lot of people in this room who look something like you? Go ahead, you think I'm kidding? Just look."

Tony is confused. Shauna thinks she might start crying, although she doesn't know why, and time seems to stop completely as she looks down at Samuel: he is still sleeping. Tony is now facing the courtroom, his face twisted in embarrassment and confusion. He looks uneasily at Shauna.

Shauna realizes he feels betrayed. She convinced him that their agreement would be well received; that the court would thank them for working things out, congratulate them for demonstrating responsibility by working the issues out among themselves rather than taking up the court's time. Now, she wonders if Tony might turn and flee.

The judge resolves everyone's bemusement to no one's satisfaction. "Now what do you see, young man? You see what I mean? You see that just because this pretty little thing over here who's so eager to jump up in court is probably just as eager to have you sign these papers? And all these guys looking something like you? You think you're so smart you're going to make a decision like this? Based upon what your true love told you? I don't like the smell of this arrogance, son. You don't know enough to sign away 18 years of your life."

Tony turns back around to face the judge, then over his shoulder at Shauna. She suddenly begins to understand. The judge is suggesting she is a liar. He is saying she had sex with someone besides Tony. Tony knows differently, but everyone knows exactly what the judge is insinuating. Shauna feels ashamed.

The judge is now writing on her Agreed Petition. "Here's what you all are going to do," he says, looking at no one while seeming to speak to everyone in the court. "This paperwork doesn't pass my smell test, son. So I want you and this pretty mother to go get some science. I have not just denied this motion, I've written down 'corrected for youth.' Understand? You two are going to have some blood drawn, and we are going to get some DNA and then we'll let the results tell us what we need to know. You go back to the clerk's office. They'll give you the paperwork and a date to come back here. When you have those results, Miss, bring them back in along with that pretty face, because there's no way I'll sign this boy's version of whatever you told your own daddy."

Shauna is standing now. Samuel seems to weigh 500 pounds. She wants to cry, she is thirsty, she has to use the restroom, and she knows this meant more waiting—for the clerk, for the science, for Tony, for the judge and his smell test.

Tony leaves the courtroom. Just as the door starts to close, Shauna follows behind, holding her bag, her purse, sleeping Samuel. She grasps the diaper bag as she reaches for the door and starts to make her way out of the room, into the weeks ahead, the weeks that would, she was sure, bring her the signatures, the ink, the sleep...

Samuel awakes suddenly with a hiccup. He looks at Shauna, surprised. And Shauna looks lovingly at Samuel, still teething.

Child of South Viet Nam

by Amanda Griffith and Thai Le Nguyen

Once upon a war in Viet Nam, a little 8-year-old girl walking to school or picking berries might encounter drunken soldiers, or even death. With Amanda Griffith, Thai Le Nguyen remembers.

Within the span of hundred years of human existence, what a bitter struggle is waged between genius and destiny! [Translation from Lê Xuân Thuy, Kim Vân Kiểu (page 19), Second Edition, 1968] Original poet Nguyễn-Du.

My friend Tieˆn and I stood at the base of a coconut palm in my family's orchard in an outlying Bống Son suburb. My hand ran over its coarse, grainy bark. The thick shiny leaves above blocked the view of any coconuts that had matured. On the ground a few yards away, lay fruit left by my mother and her farm workers.

I was supposed to be at home, getting ready for school.

"Thái, you always get one, and I don't," Tieˆn complained.

"They belong to my family."

I felt a pang talking to her that way. My mother never told villagers the fruits and vegetables belonged to her when she offered them gifts.

Longing for coconut milk and meat, I worked with single-minded focus, cracking the shell.

After sharing the treat with animal delight, we walked to the bridge, half a mile away. Within moments we heard distant shouting. Four people, two men and two girls in what looked like our school uniform – long white dresses and white pants – drifted toward us. As they drew closer, I could hear the men repeating some phrases, and I could see they wore the uniform of the American soldiers stationed at the base on my grandparents' property a few miles away. A neighbor who spoke some English told us later what they were saying.

"Come on. We want to meet you."

"Đêcho chúng tôi yên.". *Leave us alone.*

"We want to get to know you. Come on. Stop for a minute."

"Chúng ta phai vê nhà." *We must go home.*

I realized one of the girls was my oldest sister, Dung. The other was Thach, my second oldest sister. They broke into a run, and the Americans stumbled after them, shouting. I could tell there was something not quite right about them. Their words were slurred and they missed their steps, swaying in the gentle breeze.

My mother appeared on the porch.

"Dung, Thach, quick, inside!" She gestured with sweeping arms and clapped her hands as if willing them to escape.

Dung and Thach ran faster, and their books went flying. The soldiers were catching up when one of them, the one with a black spiky haircut, beer belly, shirt tails half out, staggered toward the pile of school books, tumbled and landed in a heap, grumbling irritably. The other, a thin man with longer, light brown hair, struggled to lift his companion by the arms. Spiky rose then crumbled, shouting what Dung later told me was "Let go!"

While Spiky attempted to stand, Tie^n hurried home, and I sneaked through the trees unnoticed. I made a dash like an angry bee to the front door.

"Hông Thái, go!" my mother ordered. "Hide in your room! Do not come out until I come for you." Her voice created panic inside me, a whirl in my stomach.

Dung and Thach burst in.

"Mother, help!" Dung cried, flying across the living room. "Two soldiers are after us."

"I know," my mother said, breathless. "Hide in Thái's room. Go in the wardrobe or under her bed and be silent. Keep your little sister quiet. Go!"

My sisters rushed in. I was standing behind the door. Thach tugged me toward the wardrobe and shoved me in, following behind me. Clothes smothered our faces, and then Dung crowded in, too. We were crammed body against body, and sweat broke out on my forehead. I heard my sisters gasping, and Dung's heart pounded against my cheek.

"Yên lang." *Don't say a word,* Dung commanded in a whisper.

Minutes later, but it seemed like an hour, I heard the soldiers bang on our door. We jumped out of the wardrobe, and I gasped. My sisters' eyes widened in fear. Dung's flashed like lightning.

Mother was screaming in Vietnamese, "Go away! Leave my house!"

We heard the soldiers hollering through the door. Then they opened it. We had no lock.

My mother continued screaming, her tone more shrill by the minute. I had never heard her sound so desperate nor so furious. We heard the Americans' boots stomping around our entry and living area, their voices booming and vulgar.

"Đi đi. Rói!" *Go away. Leave!* She kept repeating the words as if their meaning would sink through to the soldiers.

Then the front door opened again. We heard another male voice, Vietnamese.

"Leave," the voice said in English. "Go!" Someone had come to help.

I squeezed between my two taller sisters and halfway through the wardrobe door.

Dung grabbed my arm, whispering. "Hông Thái, what are you doing? Stop!"

I eased the door open a crack and slithered out. My sisters plucked up their courage and followed. My heart was thumping against my chest, like the mockingbird I had stroked once after pulling it from a trap. Our neighbor, Vinh, was circling the soldiers, flinging out his arms and yelling in English, "Leave! Leave!"

We all took the chant, and like angry bulls we jumped at them, repeating what we had heard Vinh say. "Leave, leave, leave!"

"We'll blow your heads off," the spiky-haired one thundered. "Get away from us. We just want to see them." Vinh interpreted for us later. His family had had enough money to send him to school where he had learned some English. Families stood up for each other in our village.

He continued circling, waving and shouting at them, ignoring the threat to his life.

Realizing we weren't weakening, the soldiers backed out the door, muttering. Mother ran to the window and looked out. Then she turned toward our neighbor.

"Vinh, thank you for coming to help us," she said in a quavering voice. "Who knows what they would have done if you had not come." She began to regain her calm.

Nodding as he withdrew from our house, Vinh left us to comfort each other, for by now we were all sobbing in a huddle.

Mother turned to me. "Hông Thái, what were you doing by the coconut trees? You were supposed to be getting ready for school." Her voice cracked. "When I called, you did not come." She spanked my bottom, but weakly, as though she had worked in the field all day planting vegetables.

"Girls, did you stop to talk to those men?"

"No, Mother," Dung yelled. Her face scrunched up as though like she smelled a dead rat. "They were *drunk.*"

Dung said "drunk" with a clenched jaw. I wondered what she knew about men who were "drunk." She had a whole life I didn't know about because she was ten when I was born. I was determined to ask her, but I wouldn't have a chance until that evening.

Mother walked me to school in case I encountered our American "friends" again.

"I told you to stay in your room," she said. "Why did you come out?"

"I thought you needed help."

She laughed. "Are you sure it was not because you wanted to see what was going on, you little monkey?"

Mother didn't have as much faith in human nature as Father. She was kind, but she didn't always expect kindness in return. She called it realism. Many villagers said of Father, "He is kind." Of Mother they said, "She is generous and works hard for her family."

I blushed when Mother entered the school and told the teacher of my disobedience.

"Please, remind Hông Thái not to stop and play with all the children on the way back to the village." I thought she was worried because of the soldiers. But later Thach told me she was certain they were passed out somewhere. When I asked her what "passed out" meant, she explained, "They are sleeping drunks." It sounded mysterious.

I forgot my shame as the teacher introduced a new lesson on character. We memorized most character lessons. They ranged from family values and behavior to correct actions in various situations and types of speech appropriate for different occasions.

Today's lesson was from a folk tale.

"We study folk tales for several reasons," the teacher said. "You must always realize that education and, in particular, literature should be your top priority to become the best Vietnamese citizen possible. Some people may not be able to afford education and others must work or we would have no food. But you are Vietnam's hope for our future. Folk tales teach values and how to overcome conflict. You must never let Ho Chí Minh manipulate these words for you. He uses them to his own advantage, to deride the South Vietnamese. He says the stories are crude and ignorant, but fairy tales are lessons about how to act."

I squirmed in the back of the room on my wooden bench.

"We will read 'The Dã Trang Story.'"

I loved this story. A hunter received a magic pearl from a snake he protected in the forest. The pearl gave the hunter the power to speak with animals. Because he abused the gift and became greedy, he ended up losing the gift. The teacher reinforced how Ho Chí Minh became greedy and took more and more freedom from the people and became a dictator who couldn't help anyone anymore as he did when he began politics.

Before we left school, we saluted the Vietnam flag and sang the national anthem. I looked around for my little brother, but Bân was not outside as usual. Because it was my job to bring him home, I waited. But he didn't come out of the school. Every student had gone. I reentered the school and headed for Bân's classroom. He was seated at his desk with his palms flat, and the male teacher was beating his fingertips with a ruler. Bân cried out each time the teacher struck him. As I came in, the teacher stopped.

"You must want to be a doctor when you grow up, Bân. That is all you could be with handwriting that bad. You can go now."

Tears streamed down our faces as we walked home, saddened by the sarcasm and pain inflicted on Bân. He was only 6. "When at school," my parents always told us, "the teacher becomes your parent. You owe him or her the same respect you would give to us."

The world seemed too much for me right now. The Americans, whom we thought were our friends, had attacked us. A teacher, whom we must respect no matter what, struck my brother's fingers. My world wasn't as safe as I'd thought. A sudden realization came over me. There was much for me to learn.

We walked without our usual play, and when we arrived home, I caught a glimpse of Dung reading a textbook on the living room floor. Strict and sometimes unfriendly, Dung's natural inclination was to criticize me, not to talk about anything I cared about. I loved her with a passion because I looked up to her, but I didn't know her as well as I wanted. Being the oldest, she was more an adult than everyone except Khoa, my older brother.

When she left, I entered the living room.

My curiosity overcame my usual reluctance to bother her things. I opened her textbook and saw the words: "Kim Vân Kiêu, a story about a young girl symbolic of problems in the 18th century dynasty government, written in beautiful poetry." I read, but I didn't understand much. The young girl's parents didn't have any money, so they "concubined" her. I didn't know what that meant. Kiêu, was "ravaged" and a man "revenged" her. I wandered out into the garden full of questions.

"Dung, what is a concubine?"

"Why are you asking me that?"

"I saw the story of Kiêu. You left your book open," I lied.

"Kiêu worked as a slave for her family. We study that story every year." Her eyes sparkled. If Dung liked the story, then I'd like it, I decided. I wanted to talk more, but she turned back to pick spinach for dinner. If I helped her, maybe she would keep talking.

I picked leaves and placed them in her bamboo basket. "It said a Buddhist nun saved her. I thought nuns stayed in their monastery."

"During war, nuns have to leave if it is dangerous for them. You know, I lived in a Catholic convent before you were born."

"Were you a nun?"

"No, it was Le Van An's idea for me to go there." Le Van An was my father's uncle, a bishop. "I wanted to go there to study. Father said I was so smart I should attend college. Le Van An said the best education I could get was at the convent."

"What was it like?" My heart pounded. Dung never talked to me about her life or her feelings. I kept my voice low and steady so my excitement wouldn't sidetrack her.

"Well, the nuns were serious. Maybe that is why I am like that now. They focused on religion and learning, and that was about all I did for two years. I also worked to clean and cook for them. Everyone helps with work in a convent. Even the mother superior is responsible for a chore. I scrubbed the nuns' clothes with the brush, made my own clothes, and embroidered handkerchiefs and towels."

"Did the nuns teach you the story of Kiêu?" I said to keep her talking.

"No, we just study it in high school."

"Did your teacher say good or bad things about Kiêu?" I didn't know what I was really asking. I just hoped I would find a clue to one of the unknown words.

"The story is about free will. It is about how we suffer from past sins. If we are good, we will be rewarded like Kiêu was when she married well at the end."

"She was not 'consummated'?" I asked, remembering another strange word in the text.

"No, she was not. The man she eventually married was a good man. She deserved that because she was virtuous."

I felt I understood even less now about Kiêu, but at least I could find out more about Dung.

"Did you like it in the convent?"

"Yes, I only wanted to learn to be a good daughter."

"So, why did you leave?"

She put her basket down to rest a moment and knelt in the mocha-colored dirt. The sun struck her cone hat, and the light glowed around her face.

"I would not have left if I did not have to. After the French left our country, different groups, including those following Ho Chí Minh, were trying to take control of the government. The nuns sent us home for safety." Her lips curled in a sneer when she said Ho Chí Minh's name. I didn't like to see her angry. It scared me even more than seeing American soldiers threatening us.

"I am sorry if I risked your safety today." I felt my eyes tight in their sockets and my forehead wrinkled. Would she scold me again?

"It was not your fault. I would have gone out there soon. I was afraid Mother would be hurt." She hugged me and we toppled over. And then she laughed and laughed, something unusual, even though her basket of spinach had spilled.

"Hông Thái, you are brave," she said. "That is what I like about you."

Then she was back to her normal severe self. No smile, no more hugs, no more kind words. That was her way. I held this moment close to my heart, for it could be all I would have from her. I cherished the words she'd said about me, her openness about her life, and the love she had for her family. I longed to be good like her.

I remembered what my teacher had said: "The Vietnamese can shape their own destiny." It lifted me and made me feel a little more grown up. But what was my destiny? We lived day to day, never knowing what might happen, even when we were walking home from school. Even if we went gathering berries on the mountain.

"Do not take the road," Mother warned. "Viet Cong use that route to gain power on the plains. And if you see helicopters, stand still." Her eyebrows met in a frown over the bridge of her nose, but she smiled and hugged us one at a time.

Years later, I still think she did this knowing each time she lost sight of us, she might never lay eyes on us again. She always let us go, but she sent us away with a sharp warning. She would call us her "little wandering tattlers, flying away for an adventure, only to return at night for nourishment."

On each of our arms was a small bamboo basket for gathering sweet black mountain berries on the

Thác Đá. When we returned, mother would expect our clothes to be stained with purple juice and red dirt. Mother and Tuyêt, our housekeeper, would use stiff brushes against a metal-ridged board by the well to scrub our shirts and pants sparkling white. My little hands were never needed for this work. Mother told me my main job was to stay out of trouble.

But trouble would come.

I would push it out of my mind, but it would creep into my sleep each night. The bodies lined up outside the police station each day, both villagers and Viet Cong guerillas, didn't bother me. That was normal. But until this day, never had I seen fighting up close, the actual killing. It was happening all around my home every night but under cover of darkness.

Beads of sweat trickled down my neck and back as the sun beat down on the craggy green slope. Below us, the rice paddies at the foot of the mountain sparkled like polished wood. From here, I could see the distant China Sea and its surrounding beaches. Dotting the waters, ships released scarlet smoke clouds of gunfire.

We reached a plateau and stopped to sit and rest. The villagers' thatched homes of bamboo looked like frayed cone hats. Along the road, which we had avoided for safety's sake, a familiar old woman appeared, toting a large basket like ours. She saw us and turned off the road in our direction. With her was a boy, perhaps an orphaned grandson, mounted on a water buffalo. As she walked beside him, the grandmother swatted the animal with a switch.

Thick plants and trees cloaked the mountain. We'd picked our way through, prying branches apart. This moment in the clearing was welcome. The grandmother stopped on the opposite side, glad of our presence, but not making friends.

The boy dismounted. His grandma handed him the basket and patted his head. "Hurry up and fill the basket. Come back quickly. Do not forget your way."

Seating herself on a large boulder, she wiped sweat from her face and pushed gray wisps of hair back into a tight bun at the nape of her neck. Her shoulders slumped. Half asleep in moments, she would wait for his safe return. The boy made his way back to the road, swinging his basket, his white shirt half un-tucked, his shorts baggy. His long hair hung to his shoulders, not a popular style. Probably they had no scissors.

"Should we catch up with him?" I asked, curious who the boy was even though he was Bân's age, not mine.

"No, you know we have to stay off the road," Khoa said. His tone was just like Mother's, but lately his voice had squeaked when he tried to lower it to sound authoritative. I giggled.

"Hông Thái," he fussed, "you must take this seriously. Listen to me when Mother and Father are not here."

I raced ahead, branches scratching my face and hands without my older siblings to clear them out of the way. The sun mocked my high spirits. I heard the mountain stream and wished we could play in it. When I was with the others, they wouldn't allow me to fool around. I was glad to be with them, included for once. But I felt my free spirit was chained.

We climbed for several minutes. Down on the plateau we could still see the old woman. Then I heard the familiar rumbling bee buzz of a helicopter. I curled my hand over my eyes and squinted into the sun. About a half mile away, a helicopter swooped down close to the slope, and a man hung out, looking through a cylinder attached to his machine gun. He was dressed in camouflage with a matching cap, and he wore a pair of wire-rimmed sunglasses.

We froze. No warnings from Khoa were necessary. I had it drilled into me: *Moving meant death.* "If you run," Mother would lecture at least once a week at dinner, "the helicopter will see you as enemies and will shoot you."

I faced the clearing, after checking to make sure all my brothers and sisters were with me. The grandmother sprang from her seat. She scrambled across the rocky ground toward a thick bush to her right. A big mistake. Up the road, we could no longer see the grandson. The water buffalo had been grazing. Now it snorted in agitation. With no understanding of where to find safety, the animal started running.

The grandmother raced toward the brush.

The soldier who leaned out darted back into the helicopter as it swept in her direction. She screamed like a cornered mountain cat, and he opened fire.

The soil around the grandmother's feet erupted in dusty haze, as the gunfire chewed and pitted the earth.

Her head flew to the side, a red ball trailing a ribbon of blood. An arm was hurled into the brush. The bullets gouged gaping flaps in her stomach. I felt vomit rise from my stomach. We could do nothing, and I knew if we moved a muscle, we would be the next targets.

The shooting lasted less than a minute, but for me it dragged on as if in slow motion. The helicopter came in close, searching for any other movement. We stood like statues as it snaked along the slope.

I moved my foot for better balance.

Thach hissed, "It is not safe yet. Do not move!"

I stood, breathing and blinking only, thinking only of home.

A few minutes later, the helicopter flew off and we were alone. We talked about what to do.

"Should we try to move her to town?" Dung asked Khoa.

"No one could expect us to carry the bloody pieces back to the village." Khoa's voice was edged with a low rasp, unlike the squeaking that had made me laugh earlier.

"Can we still pick berries?" Nga, my second youngest sister, asked. "I do not think they will come back."

"Nga, a woman was just *killed*," Dung said.

"I know, but we did not cause it, and we can not help her."

"It would be disrespectful not to honor her and leave her in peace," Khoa said.

We began our somber descent. No swinging baskets or light chatter lifted our hearts. Down we climbed, stepping over rough and rocky paths and sweeping brush aside with our hands as we went. We looked around for the boy as we headed down, hoping we would see him. But in our shaken state we were desperate to get home. There was no sign of him.

I drifted down the mountain in a trance, but when I saw our home, I woke up. Our house was the one high place in the flood of sadness. We raced into the kitchen, where Mother and Tuyêt stood together, preparing the midday meal of shrimp and noodles for themselves and the workers who picked squash in our garden. Mother saw us first and flinched as if hit in the face. She stopped stirring the pot of shrimp, the wooden spoon clutched in her hand.

"What happened? Where are your berries?" she said, her eyes wide and anxious.

"A helicopter shot down that grandmother! The one who has the water buffalo and the rice field near the bridge on the Thác Đá side"

"Was anyone hurt?" We knew she meant us.

"The boy climbed up to pick berries. He was not hurt." Khoa said. "The grandmother ran. She was blown to pieces."

Mother's wooden spoon clattered to the floor.

"We stood still, Mother. We all stood absolutely still."

Mother looked at us. Then she moved toward us, her face twisted with emotion, and spread her arms wide. I sucked in my breath and she gathered us in a huge embrace.

That night Mother came into my room to make sure I was in bed as usual. Outside, grenades and gunfire provided the background for sleep. She came to my bed and knelt beside me for the first time since I was small. Tears fell from her huge dark eyes, but her expression was calm.

"Mother, I stood still. I did what you told me," I said.

She folded me in her arms. "Little one, you were a good daughter." She stroked my hair. "You *are* a good daughter."

Outside, the guns banged and boomed, somehow comforting us because we were used to them.

We never saw or heard of the boy again and didn't know what became of him, though we asked everywhere. We hoped and prayed he was with some aunt or uncle or adopted by a nice Vietnamese family. Family is of the highest importance and, as Christmas approached, my family drew closer and closer together to heal our painful memories with our love for each other.

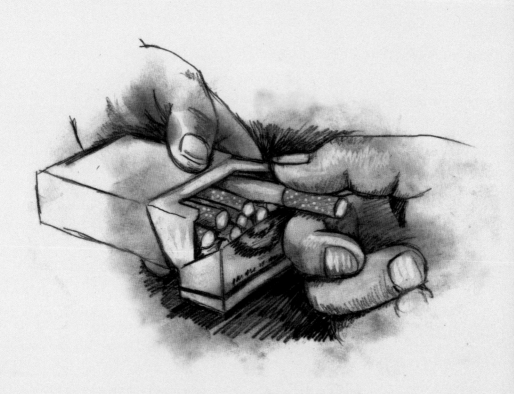

A Cigarette on the Champs-Élysées

by Evan Moore

It is the most famous street in the most beautiful city in the world, the Avenue des Champs-Élysées, a mile and a quarter of architectural wonder and opulence that crosses through the heart of Paris.

For more than 400 years, the rich and poor, the best and worst have traveled along the granite blocks that form that magnificent thoroughfare. It extends less than a mile and a quarter, runs northwest to connect the Place de la Concorde to Napoleon Bonaparte's Arc de Triomphe, but it leads its travelers in whatever direction they choose.

I found myself on the Champs-Élysées during the Christmas season of 1997. It was the year in which Princess Diana of Wales died in Paris in a fiery crash in the Pont de 'Alma tunnel, the year that Ira Einhorn was arrested and the year I turned 50 and quit smoking. It was Einhorn, "The Unicorn," who brought me to France. I was there on assignment, writing a story about the man whose 16-year international cat and mouse game with police had come to an end.

Einhorn was larger than life, both repulsive and fascinating. An icon of the 1960s, he was a mysterious genius, a guru, a grand charlatan and, ultimately, a murderer. He hailed from Philadelphia, where he had been an impressive student in high school in the 1950s and an outstanding football player, good enough that he was awarded a scholarship to the University of Pennsylvania. Einhorn, however, was *difficult*. At the university, professors marveled at his intellect but were frustrated by his aggressive personality. Always ahead of his time, he "turned on, tuned in and dropped out" years before Timothy Leary coined the phrase in 1967.

In 1961, Einhorn left Philadelphia and traveled to California, where he mixed with the growing radical element in Berkeley and Palo Alto. By the time he returned to City of Brotherly Love in 1964, he was a credentialed initiate of the long-haired counterculture, one who had taken LSD with Ken Kesey, studied Eastern religions and preached the religious aspects of marijuana. He assumed the nickname "The Unicorn," derived from the translation of his German-Jewish surname, and he spoke the language of hippies long before it was heard in the mainstream. He had qualities that made him an anomaly in mid-1960s Philadelphia, and he soon found a way to manipulate them to his advantage. Einhorn fed off audacity. Quick-witted and charming, he was also insulting, burly and overbearing. Having conned his way into a position as an adjunct teacher of metaphysics at his alma mater, he once stripped naked in class and danced around the room while smoking marijuana. He dominated most conversations and was usually the center of attention. His bushy hair and beard were often uncombed, he bathed irregularly and his body odor was prevalent. Nonetheless, his eyes reflected a burning intelligence. He seduced numerous women with his wit and won men over with his intellect.

Most of the time, Einhorn proudly managed to live without ever working at any actual job. Others supported him. By the early 1970s, he had established himself as the leading spokesman for Philadelphia's hippies, a teacher at the University of Pennsylvania's Free University and a New Age guru who aggressively preached pacifism. His circle of friends included the cream of the counterculture—among them, Jerry Rubin, Abbie Hoffman, Alvin Toffler and Allen Ginsberg. He had created a network of intellectuals for which he served as the hub and dubbed himself "a planetary enzyme." He was on the cutting edge of the youth movement, was master of ceremonies at Earth Day in 1970 and ran a satirical race for mayor of Philadelphia in 1971. Always on someone else's tab, he regaled audiences in his sparse apartment and at his favorite French restaurant, La Terrasse, near his alma mater.

He was holding court at La Terrasse when he met Holly Maddux in 1972. It was a beauty and the beast pairing. Maddux was Einhorn's opposite. Blond, beautiful, with striking Arian features, she was a product of East Texas, where she had been a high school cheerleader in Tyler, graduated salutatorian and was voted "most likely to succeed" in her class of 1965. A talented dancer and a sharp student, she was quiet, polished and reserved, hiding her feelings behind a Mona Lisa smile. That smile, however, masked a deep dissatisfaction with small-town East Texas. After graduation, she passed up proffered scholarships to Texas schools and left for Bryn Mawr College in Pennsylvania, then traveled in Europe and Israel after graduation there. Despite her education and ability, she never settled on an occupation but floated from one location and job to another. By 1972, she had worked her way to Philadelphia and Ira Einhorn. They were in bed within an hour of their first visit, Einhorn later boasted, and within days, Maddux had moved in with the guru. That began a stormy, five-year relationship during which Einhorn alternately dominated, abused, courted and supplicated Maddux. For her part, Maddux often defied Einhorn, but seemed drawn to him. Periodically, she left him, but never with conviction and always to return.

That is until the summer of 1977. That summer Einhorn and Maddux toured England, where Einhorn spoke to groups researching paranormal, psychic theories. The couple fought repeatedly. Toward the end of the trip, Maddux wrote her family that she had decided to leave Einhorn. Then, shortly after she and Einhorn returned to Philadelphia, she disappeared. Einhorn said she left. Maddux's family, fearing the worst, reported her missing. But Philadelphia police gave perfunctory treatment to the case, believing she was a grown woman who had set out on her own. Her relatives persisted, however, and hired a private investigator. Almost two years after she had vanished, the investigator convinced police to search Einhorn's apartment. On April 28, 1979, investigators opened a padlocked closet on Einhorn's porch and found a locked steamer trunk inside. In the trunk was the mummified body of Holly Maddux, shrunken to 37 pounds. She had been beaten to death, suffered at least a dozen skull fractures and a broken jaw.

Einhorn was charged with murder and his defense was characteristically outrageous. He had been keeping sensitive documents from behind the Iron Curtain in the trunk, he said. Sinister forces, including the CIA and the KGB (apparently working in unison), had killed Maddux, removed the documents and placed her body in the trunk to implicate him. The case was the talk of Philadelphia, and Einhorn's bond hearing was almost a social event. With Arlen Specter (later to become U.S. Senator Arlen Specter) as his attorney and a host of influential character witnesses, Einhorn was freed on $40,000 bail, using his mother's house as collateral.

On Jan. 13, 1981, the day his trial was to begin, he was nowhere to be found. Einhorn became a fugitive. Eventually he was spotted in Dublin, Ireland, a country that had no extradition agreement with the U.S. He began hop-scotching around Europe. Aided by funds from his wealthy friends, among them Barbara Bronfman, then-wife of Charles Bronfman, heir to the Seagram's fortune in

Canada, Einhorn bounced around Europe for years.

In 1993, he was tried in absentia in Philadelphia and convicted of Maddux's murder. By then he had begun living in England with Annika Flodin, daughter of a wealthy Swedish family with interests in the fashion industry. It is unclear whether Flodin knew of Einhorn's fugitive status, but she *did* assume an alias. Supported by Flodin's wealth, the couple moved to the remote French wine country village of Champagne-Mouton, where they purchased a historic mill that had been converted to a home. They assimilated well. Flodin was popular in town, regarded as a sort of "earth mother" with a ready smile, a woman who baked her own bread and was environmentally conscious. Einhorn, using the name "Eugene Mallon," was rarely seen, spoke no French and conversed only with the few English-speaking residents and members of a bridge club he joined. Members of the club found him unpleasant. But he was a good bridge player, so they tolerated him. He seemed content to remain in his house and work with the elaborate computer system he had installed there.

Then, in June, 1997, Annika Flodin registered her automobile in her real name. Knowing that Einhorn was living with Flodin, police noted the address on the registration, and Einhorn was arrested and jailed, briefly. Supported by Flodin's family, Einhorn hired attorney Dominique Delthil of Bordeaux, one of France's finest, and Delthil fought extradition. Appealing to the French disdain for the death penalty, he contended that barbarous American courts would inflict death on Einhorn, whose only crime was social dissidence. French courts sided with Delthil, citing Einhorn's trial in absentia. Einhorn was released on personal recognizance and, once again, appeared to have beaten the odds.

The story appealed to me. I had read Steven Levy's excellent book, *The Unicorn's Secret,* about the murder and Einhorn's flight. I also had a tenuous connection to the Maddux family. My wife had known Holly and her siblings as a child and had introduced me to Holly Maddux's sister, Buffy. I also held an enviable position with the Houston Chronicle. Shrinking ad revenues had not yet crippled newspapers. I had found a niche as a "writer at large" and was given great leeway with stories. I had earned it, I thought. For years I had started early and quit late, written and rewritten and agonized over every turn of phrase. My efforts had paid off. The editors had confidence in me and allowed me to pursue the stories I chose. I had built my foundation well.

So, I packed for France. All I brought was clothes, passport, pens, notebooks, computer and the ever-present package of Marlboro Reds. Having turned 50, I had resolved to quit smoking but, having lied to myself for years as I puffed away, I found that I had to lie to myself to stop it. The idea that I would never again touch a cigarette was overwhelming, austere, too much to bear. I had not "quit" cigarettes, I told myself. I simply hadn't smoked one in a while. To assure myself of that fact, I kept a package in my breast pocket at all times.

Once in Lyon, I set about gathering information and arranging interviews. My job, I decided, was to do more than just interview all the characters. It was to find out what Einhorn's life was like in France, to talk to as many people as possible who had contact with him and to try to talk to Einhorn, as well. I had little hope for the latter. Since his arrest, Einhorn had refused all requests for interviews from American journalists. We knew too much about his past. I also faced another hurdle. My French was terrible and Champagne Mouton was deep in the wine region of the south. Few spoke English in that area, and I knew I would need help. I soon enlisted a young French journalist as an interpreter and guide, a freelancer from Paris who was intrigued by the story and accompanied me on most of my interviews.

The story seemed to fall together. I found Einhorn's attorney, the judge in his case, city officials and town residents who knew The Unicorn. I even tracked down members of his bridge club. Time and again, I heard the French question the justice of a trial in absentia, of the inherent danger in the American penchant for the death penalty, the possibility that Einhorn was telling the truth and was innocent. I took it in stride and politely did the interviews. I wasn't in France to question the French attitude toward justice, only to report on it.

At the same time, I gathered information on Einhorn. I located his home just outside town. Like many of the buildings in the town, it appeared to be at least 400 years old, a two-story stone structure with a gated drive and well-tended flower gardens at the front. I also learned what I believed had drawn The Unicorn to Champagne Mouton. Ancient, quaint and secluded, it was an idyllic French town, but not one that drew many tourists. Open-air bistros dotted its cobble-stoned streets. Residents walked their dogs along its walkways in the crisp, December air. Children played in its park. Each Wednesday, a farmers market was set up in the square, where locally grown produce, chickens, pigs and bread were sold. "Eugene Mallon" and Annika were often seen shopping at the market. I decided to stake them out on friendly turf. Encountering them in public would be better than knocking on an unanswered door at the mill. I was certain that if I made an initial attempt at the home, I would never come face to face with Einhorn.

Wednesday arrived, and my guide and I parked ourselves in a cafe with a clear view of the market. It was clear and bright, almost balmy for December, and the square was bustling. As we drank coffee and watched the commerce, I thought about the story I had come to write. I had reached the point of research that was always bittersweet to me. I had everything except Einhorn, and I didn't really need him, or so I thought. I didn't want to create an ugly scene in this quiet little town, which was entirely possible. I also had no desire to listen to his ridiculous alibi, even if he was willing to talk to me. Einhorn was no fool, and that would work in my favor. He would undoubtedly turn me down if he didn't take a swing at me. Still, l had to make an effort to speak to him. That's how I had been trained. It's what professional journalists do.

Then, they were there. Annika Flodin, smiling, slight, blond, freckled, wearing a light coat and jeans, and beside her, The Unicorn. He was lighter than he had been in his youth, his legs almost bandy, almost thin in a pair of denim shorts. The hair had gone white and was now trimmed closely, the beard trimmed. Yet it was unmistakably him. The eyes, with their intense stare, were unchanged. As we stepped from the cafe and moved toward them, those eyes rose and met mine. There was an immediate reaction. He did not know me, but he instantly knew who I was. He knew from my appearance that I was no French local, that I was headed in his direction and he wanted nothing to do with me. Quickly, he grabbed Flodin's arm and hustled her from the market. They walked briskly to a small car, parked nearby and jumped in.

"Hurry, get the car," I told my guide, as I moved to the corner to see which way they went. My guide was back in a moment. I jumped in the passenger seat and the pursuit began. As we sped out of Champagne Mouton with Einhorn barely in view, I realized that he was heading back to the converted mill. "Keep after him," I said. "They'll stop." He and Flodin arrived at their home just as we were catching up to them, and I could see Einhorn scuttling from the car toward the front door, with Flodin behind him. My guide pulled up at the entrance and stopped. I saw that, in their haste, they had not shut and locked their front gate.

"Wait," I told him. "I'm going in."

"NO," my guide said. "You can't do that in France. It's trespass."

"I don't care," I said. "I didn't come all the way from Texas to stop at the front gate."

I walked to the front door and knocked. There was no answer. I knocked again. I stepped back and yelled, "Mr. Einhorn. My name is Evan Moore. I am a writer for the *Houston Chronicle*, and I would like to talk to you."

A face appeared at an open upstairs window, but it was not Einhorn's. The eyes that looked at me were not the burning orbs that had spotted me in the market. They were Annika Flodin's eyes, soft, pitiful and brimming with tears.

"We know who you are," she said, in accented English. "Please, please go away. My husband will not talk to you. Go away. Go away."

I watched her face recede from the window. I turned and headed back to the car. I had done my job. I had chased Einhorn to his retreat, and now I could write a tale of a man who beat one woman to death, only to hide behind the skirts of another. I felt good, satisfied, pleased with myself and only slightly cruel. Still, Annika Flodin's eyes followed me onto the bullet train to Paris the next day. They blinked at me in tear-filled angst as my interpreter and I played gin rummy in the club car. They rode with me in the taxi to my hotel and up the elevator to my room.

Finally, I dismissed them. "The woman is a fool," I thought. "She made her own bed, and now she can lie in it. These French people, with their gorgeous cities, their excellent food, their amazing art and their wonderful wine, they're foolish as well. *If they can listen to this bombastic bastard with his ridiculous tales of the CIA and the KGB, they're just not as discerning as I am.* I turned my thoughts to my one night in Paris. I would not have time to see the Louvre nor many of the other things I would have visited as a tourist. I had to be in London the next day to begin work on another story. I could, however, see one sight: the Champs-Élysées at its most beautiful.

I had read of the street many times. More than just a modern wonder, it dates to 1616, when Marie de Medici decided to plant trees along the path to the Tuileries Gardens. The path later became the Champs-Élysées, named for the Greek Elysian Fields, the burial ground for heroes. Over the years, it was widened and, because of the many historic landmarks along its path, it became the primary route for parades and celebrations in Paris. Today, the avenue is a special part of city in the weeks leading to Christmas, and it is decorated as only the French can. In the evening, its wide lanes are closed to vehicular traffic and hordes of shoppers wander freely up and down its streets. Along the sidewalks, the carefully trimmed horse-chestnut trees are filled with lights that resemble snowflakes. The shops and restaurants are all decorated, and music can be heard playing from various clubs.

With the Champs-Élysées as my destination, I slipped on my overcoat, felt for my cigarettes and my card case in the left breast pocket and headed out to the avenue. I took a cab from my hotel. The driver was loquacious and began pointing out sights as we passed them. As we reached the Pont de 'Alma road tunnel, he gestured toward a long, jagged scar on one of the concrete walls.

"That's where it happened," he said. "Right there is where Princess Diana and her boyfriend died, where they were chased to their death by the paparazzi."

Once again I thought of Annika Flodin. But we were nearing my destination and the cab came to a stop. I stepped out and into an exotic environment. It was the most brilliant lighting display I had ever seen. I began walking, still buoyed by the self-satisfaction of having wrapped up a good story. All along the thoroughfare, people seemed happy, festive. I heard laughter and music. I reveled in the scents of the avenue. I passed a *parfumerie* and the overwhelming, almost cloyingly sweet smell of perfume filled the cold night air. That was offset by the familiar aroma of smoke from a fine cigar. Unlike America, the French had no trade embargo with Cuba and Cuban cigars were available.

I looked across the street at a small *Tabac* shop and spotted the source of the aroma. A man was near the shop door and had just lit what appeared to be a large panatela. The scent was intoxicating. I felt the cigarettes in my pocket. I didn't want a cigarette. I wanted a cigar. After all, I had just completed a yeoman's job. I deserved one. I walked into the shop and bought a long, black Cuban Robusto. I bit off the end and had just stepped outside to light up when I noticed someone in front of me.

He was a small man, shorter than I, maybe 30 and rather nondescript with a slightly olive complexion and brown hair. He was wearing what appeared to be a leather jacket that could have been either very expensive or a good imitation. And he was looking at me with an almost mocking smile.

"Say," he said. "Give me a cigarette." The words might have been spoken with some accent, but it was slight. The smile was wider now, however, clearly insolent, and the statement was an order, not a request.

"I don't think so," I said, with a smile that I hoped was equally insulting as I stepped around him. I took two steps, and he was there again, this time with his hand on my arm.

"I said, 'Give me a cigarette,' American," he said.

"Get your hand off me and get away from me," I told him and muscled by him, heading to the curb and a side street intersection. I stepped off the curb and, suddenly, he was there again, immediately in front of me. I stumbled over him, and he seemed to stumble backward as well and clutched at my coat. We staggered across the street like two drunken dancers, almost falling. Once across, he let go and I regained my balance. I looked at him, still mocking me with that grin, and I was suddenly angry.

I grabbed his jacket, slammed him against a light pole and, for a moment, was about to ram my fist into his smirking face when something stopped me.

"Look," I said. "I don't want to hurt you. Just get the hell away from me and leave me alone." I let him go, and he backed away and into the crowd without a word. I stood there for a moment, straightening my clothes and was about to walk back down the avenue when he appeared in front of me again.

"Be careful, my friend," he said. "Paris is a city of thieves."

He reached into his jacket pocket, pulled out my card case and handed it to me. I stared at it in shock, and he backed away, smiled again, waved and was lost in the crowd. My French francs were in that wallet, my passport, all my credit cards. My stomach sank with the instant realization that he had picked my pocket. I had just been taken, duped. I was a mark. That man was mocking me, alright. He wanted me to know it and had stolen me blind. Slowly, I opened the wallet and, with a sick feeling, looked inside.

It was all there. My passport, my cards, my French francs, my Texas driver's license, the picture of my son smiling back at me. Nothing was missing, nothing touched. I stared for a moment in disbelief, then tried to catch sight of the little man again. He was nowhere to be seen. I began retracing my path down the avenue. My self-satisfaction shattered, I walked at least a half-block before I realized I was still smoking the cigar. I needed to reflect on what had just occurred. I stepped into a small, crowded bar and ordered a brandy. I sipped it and wondered: What just happened? Why did that man pick my pocket, only to give my wallet back to me? *Who was he? What was he?*"

Just to my right, I noticed a May-September couple eyeing me. The woman was young, pretty. The man was older, distinguished. They were obviously a couple and had been one long enough to reach a plateau of complacency with one another. The man leaned toward me and smiled.

"Pardon me," he said in a strong, French accent. "You are American? My wife does not speak English, but she wonders."

"Yes," I replied.

"My wife would like to ask, 'What do you think of Paris?'"

I hesitated for a moment before telling them what had just happened. As I recounted the tale and the husband translated, I watched the woman's expressions. Interest, surprise, incredulity, then deep consideration.

"I can't figure this out," I told them. "This man had to be a pickpocket, a thief. But why would he give my wallet back to me? Who in the hell is he?"

The older man smiled and shrugged. "Who knows?" he said. "Strange things happen in Paris."

I left for London the next morning, riding in a cab past the Avenue des Champs-Élysées, past the beautiful streets and architecture that form Paris, past the Louvre and past the jagged scar in the concrete wall of the Pont de 'Alma road tunnel. I thought of Princess Diana who died there, chased by a crowd of paparazzi and chauffeured by a drunken driver. I thought of the tears in Annika Flodin's eyes and wondered how much I had in common with those paparazzi. I thought of the man who had picked my pocket, and I thought of Einhorn. I knew I had learned something, but I wasn't sure what.

It took years for that lesson to jell. It was nothing new. Robert Burns knew it centuries before when he wrote *To a Mouse*. Uncertainty reigns supreme. *"The best laid schemes o' Mice an' Men, Gang aft agley."*

For four years after I chased him from the market in Champagne Mouton, Ira Einhorn basked in self assurance. He thumbed his nose at American courts, appeared on television shows to proclaim his innocence and sipped wine while posing naked for photographers in the garden of his converted mill house.

That all ended in July, 2001, when Einhorn was extradited and tried again in Philadelphia. Initially, he cut his own throat but failed to kill himself and recovered. Months later he received a life sentence.

The niche I thought was so secure began to crumble a few years later as the creeping miasma of declining newspaper profits found its way to Houston. Long, in-depth features were icing on the cake for newspapers. "Writers at large" became expendable. Faced with shrinking parameters I left the job I had spent the better part of my adult life building and sought a new career.

Diana never intended to die in that tunnel.

I'll probably never know what became of the man who picked my pocket. I'll probably never see him again. I'm not certain, however. I'll never be *certain* again.

If I do see him, I'll hand him one of my Marlboro Reds.

Red Stilettos

by Iris Podolsky

I hated my wedding. It's fifty years later, and I still can't help thinking back to my sister Lily's wedding with envy in my heart. It wasn't about the venue, the dress or the food. My wedding was far more elaborate than Lily's.

My jealousy is about my father.

Every young girl needs the protection and support of her father when choosing a life partner. Just as my father shrewdly appraised Philip Bogdonoff when he came to court my sister Lily, he would have loved probing the incisive intelligence of the young medical student who came for me. But it was not to be.

And so on my wedding day my heart ached for the father who was not there to give me away. It was not enough having a loving step-father take his place. I wanted my Daddy.

My father almost didn't make Lily's wedding, either. Though Dad was mortally ill, he played just as instrumental a role as Ma did in Lily and Philip's union. Their romance had an interesting start, seasoned with a dash of old world charm.

***

"Mr. Katz, do you have any brains today?" Ma said into the phone to our butcher, oblivious to the ambiguity of her question. "It's Sara Bloom from Camden. I'm coming over to Philly today for some veal chops for my husband...you remember Red Bloom? Well, he's been very sick lately but has a yen for a nice thick veal chop tonight. I need the brains for tomorrow's lunch, but since Fourth Street Farmer's Market is such a schlepp, I thought I'd kill two birds with one stone.

"Excellent. You know, Mr. Katz, I only come to you for my kosher meat because I know what I'm getting. So save your brains and I'll see you this afternoon."

Ma hung up the phone and turned to me. "Iris, get your jacket. We'll stop by Green Valley for a milkshake on the way."

I ignored Ma's peace offering. "Do we have to spend an hour there like last time with all the yentas at the butcher shop?"

"Listen, Missy, a little respect. You should never know from what those women have suffered through."

Mr. Katz's Kosher Butcher Shop was packed wall-to-wall with "battleships," as my brother-in-law calls the yentas. Just as Ma and I squeezed onto the wooden bench in front of the immaculate meat cases to wait our turn, a buxom woman with a startlingly white pageboy gave my cheek a crippling pinch. I was fascinated by her fleshy upper arm, which quivered beneath her short-sleeved dress. Hadassah arms, Ma calls them. I call them batwings. Glancing down, I saw the ubiquitous tan elastic stockings and American Girl lace-up shoes wildly popular in 1953 that made matrons of a certain age look like they stepped out of the chorus line at Minsky's Burlesque.

"Kenahora, what a shayna maidel!" the woman crooned, giving my mother a congratulatory nod of her pageboy.

"I've got three more beauties, all older than this kleininkha—two already married," Ma crowed with pride. "I only have my Lily and this 8-year-old at home now. I'm Sara Bloom and you are Mrs...?'

"Oy vey, forgive my rudeness. I'm Mrs. Bogdonoff from South Philadelphia by Snyder Avenue. Are you from the neighborhood? I haven't seen you before."

"I come over from Camden to shop. My husband is very sick, a bad heart, but he enjoys a nice piece of veal every now and then. Tomorrow I'm making brains in brown butter for a luncheon, so I needed to see Mr. Katz. Who else can you rely on for fresh brains?"

"You're so lucky with your daughters, so beautiful, I bet, like this shanekite." Mrs. Bogdonoff gave my other cheek a terrifying twist. "I, too, have four children, all sons, all married except for the youngest. He's already 28 years old with not a woman in sight. Vey, my heart aches for him. And so handsome he is, tall with shining red hair, like mine when I was a girl." She sighed, smoothing her snow-white coif.

"An educated man, a malamed, a high school teacher, my Philip. What is he waiting for?" she complained. "For me to croak so he can throw himself away on some gentile, some shiksa? How could it be there's no nice Jewish girl for him? You think I exaggerate? Here, look at his picture." She fumbled in her purse for her wallet.

"Just like my husband, with the wavy red hair," Ma clucked. "Yes, by God, a beautiful boy with goodness written all over his face, just like my Lily."

From out of the purse Ma brandished Lily's high school photo for Mrs. Bogdonoff, who made a little whistling sound through the gap between her two front teeth.

 "A real beauty you got there, Mrs. Bloom. So nu, she has a young man calling?"

"She's got plenty of admirers but no one steady. She's only seventeen, my Lily, but bright as a new penny. Already she's taking up stenography and typing for a job in the secretarial pool in a downtown law firm. And a homemaker, a balabusta like you've never seen. When she cleans the kitchen floor, you can eat lunch on it," Ma announced.

"Well, we need to do something about this, Mrs. Bloom. I've got the son, you've got the daughter, let's see if we can make a shidduch. What do you think? You'll give me your telephone number for my Philip. What do we have to lose?"

The other battleships, who had been listening in, nodded in synchronized approval, and Mr. Katz called Ma's number.

"Mrs. Bogdonoff, it's been a pleasure." Ma grinned conspiratorially as if they'd just concluded the Warsaw Pact.

***

Seven months went by with no phone call from Philip Bogdonoff. Lily's indignation over Ma's matchmaking had totally dissipated. Then one Sunday afternoon, the phone rang. Ma picked up the receiver. A devilish smile played over her face.

"Lily! Lillian. Come to the phone," she yelled upstairs to the bathroom, where my sister spent most of her free time.

"Who is it, Ma?"

"It's Calvin Coolidge. Come down."

As Lily bounded down the steps, she gave Ma a quizzical look and a lift of her finely chiseled chin. Her dark hair bounced against her freckled face, a red-headed complexion unusual on a brunette. Lily was a younger version of Ma at the time, busty with generous curves but taller. Five-foot-one is statuesque for the women in our family.

"Hello? Yes, this is Lily Bloom. Who's this again?

"Your mother and my mother did *what*?" she shouted into the receiver. Then she stopped for a moment to catch her breath and glare at Ma.

"I *am* calm. Look, I'm sure you're a very nice man and probably not used to your mother arranging a blind date for you by Mr. Katz, the butcher, either. This reminds me of the shtetles in Europe where the matchmakers get together over the photos… No, thank you, this is not the way I do things. But thanks for calling."

She turned to Ma. "If you ever do that again, I'm going to kill you. This is not the old country with marriages arranged by Yenta the Matchmaker. If I were an old girl, say 20, that's one thing. But Ma, I'm just 17. What were you thinking?"

"Listen, my darling, you start talking with someone at the butcher shop. She shows you her pictures, you show her yours. You figure, what's the harm? He's a good-looking young professional, a school teacher from Philadelphia. Just because he got your number from me instead of one of your friends doesn't mean he's a bad person. Forget about it. Anyway, he won't call back with that razor sharp tongue of yours."

But he did. And just a few days later. As Ma listened in on the downstairs extension, I tried to eavesdrop with Lily. This time she broke up laughing. What was he saying? *How about a nice veal chop? Do you have any brains today?* By the time Lily got off the phone she was in stitches.

Leaning into me, she giggled. "Maybe he's not so bad, this Philip Bogdonoff."

"So, did he ask you out?" I quizzed, fascinated with the ins and outs of the dating game.

"Yes, and to some fancy Philadelphia supper club Saturday night. What am I going to tell Ma?"

"She already heard. When you picked up here, she ran for the extension in the kitchen."

***

Saturday afternoon began with the endless rigmarole of washing, pressing, tweezing, waxing and polishing. Personally, I'd rather have been on my scooter or reading a book. I could never see myself fussing so much for a dinner.

I hid behind the upstairs banister when the doorbell rang promptly at 7:30. Ma answered with her usual aplomb, silently appraising Philip Bogdonoff as he stepped into our foyer. Lily waited to make her dramatic entrance, of course. As she swept down the stairs in a red sheath dress with a large silk flower at the cinched waist, her dyed-to-match six-inch pumps clicked lightly on the steps. From the second floor, I peered over the rail to gauge the effect of her appearance on the hapless victim. No doubt about it. He was struck by "Lil lightning." Even I had to admit my otherwise obnoxious sister looked dishy.

And not a goober, this Philip Bogdonoff. But there it was when he smiled, that comic gap between his two front teeth, just like his mother's. He was tall and slender with red hair like our Dad's. Tall was a big thing in our family.

"A blind date, arranged by our mothers. Not promising. Philip could barely get his words together coherently. "You sounded nice on the phone but I didn't expect…" His eyes slid appreciatively over my sister's fabulous figure in that red dress.

"Neither did I," Lil answered, returning his stare. "You made me laugh on the phone. That's why I accepted." For a minute they stood there like two dummies, in disbelief at their mothers' canny machinations.

Watching from the dining room, Ma sighed with deep satisfaction, her right hand resting on her generous bosom. "Twelve o'clock, just like Cinderella, Philip. Lily, take a wrap for the night air."

"Yes, Mrs. Bloom. I'll have her back on the dot." He flashed a flushed, lop-sided grin as he held the door open, drinking Lily in from her creamy, freckled shoulders all the way down to the red stilettos.

Ma moved the curtain away from the window to peer out to the street as Philip held the car door open for Lily. "Not bad, not bad at all, Irisel," she said, half to herself. "Polite, clean-cut, starched shirt, shined shoes. What do you think?"

I was hardly any judge of a suitor's credentials, but Ma seemed impressed.

Later that night, I heard my sister's laughter by the front door just as our grandfather clock struck the witching hour. Ma was rustling around the bedroom, unable to wait for the usual Sunday brunch recap. Rubbing the sleep from my eyes, I couldn't wait either.

"So nu, Mrs. Lincoln, aside from the shooting, how was the show?" quizzed Ma. Judging from my sister's face, I reckoned the show was a hit, in spite of the producers.

"He's smart, Ma, and funny. I've not met anyone like him."

"Considering your vast experience, Lily, that's not hard to imagine. He's more mature than the others, so be careful. This is not a teenager but a grown man you're fooling with. And from South Philly, no less," she added skeptically.

"Wait. Now *you're* leery Ma?" Lily said sharply. "Why did you give him my number in the first place if you thought he was too old for me?"

"I might have gotten swept up in the moment at the butcher shop," Ma admitted. "It was a long shot that he might call anyway. After all, he's almost eleven years older. Maybe not such a good idea. Are you seeing him again?"

"Yes, I am. Next Sunday he invited me to a picnic and a swim in Atlantic City. Now don't tell me I can't go." The pleasure of the evening had suddenly vanished from Lily's face.

The following Sunday, Dad, Ma and I sat like statues in the living room waiting for Philip Bogdonoff. Lily was upstairs as usual when the doorbell rang, this time fussing with baby oil, sunglasses, and a change of clothes. Philip walked in carrying a 5-pound box of Barton's chocolates for Ma, his hand outstretched in greeting to my father. In striped bathrobe and slippers, Dad rose with difficulty from his favorite wingchair.

"Please, Mr. Bloom. Sit. Don't trouble yourself. I understand you haven't been well lately. Is there anything I can do?" Philip added.

"No, but I did want to meet you after my wife's glowing report. I understand you teach school in Philly?"

"Yes, English. I'm studying for my master's degree in education. One day I hope to apply for vice principal and maybe even principal of my high school."

Dad smiled. Because of his bad heart, Dad never had the opportunity for higher education. Nothing pleased him more than an ambitious, well-educated man.

"You know, our Lily is not yet out of high school herself. I trust you will treat her with the utmost respect. She's a good girl and I want her to stay that way. Do we understand each other?" Dad was not one for pulling punches.

Just then Lily entered the room in dazzling white short-shorts and a sunflower yellow halter top. "Ah, Phil, I see you've met my father."

Philip sprang up from the ottoman at the sound of her voice, and his eyes met Lily's.

"Where exactly are we going this afternoon? I put everything but the kitchen sink in my beach bag." Lil tossed the oversized hamper nonchalantly on the chair as she leaned in to plant a kiss on Dad's forehead.

Red-faced, Philip noisily cleared his throat. "Actually we're going to Margate. Our cousin's club is having a gathering at my Aunt Yetta's house. You'll be able to change there after we swim. My mother and aunts cook for days for these family get-togethers. There's always a huge spread, usually barbecue with some Russian specialties thrown in. Is that okay?"

Now it was Lily's turn to look red-faced. "I didn't realize we were going to a family outing. Maybe I should change to a sundress, Ma. What do you think?" Lily turned to Ma, who had turned her attention to Barton's famous butter creams.

"Thank you so much, Philip. How did you know this is my favorite?" Ma said, sinking her teeth into a luscious confection.

"Ma, what do you think?" Lily repeated, trying to get Ma's attention. "I didn't realize we were visiting relatives at the shore, your whole family at that. I...I," Lily seemed stuck for the moment.

"Mom's five sisters and all my young cousins will be there. They're great fun. You'll see," he said encouragingly.

"Famous last words," remarked Lily under her breath.

Dad nodded his approval while Ma squeezed a butter cream to determine whether the filling was chocolate mousse or raspberry cream.

Lily looked dismayed but gathered her things.

***

Later, my sister would tell me how the events that day unfolded.

"Why didn't you tell me this was your cousin's club?" she complained to Philip as they pulled up to Aunt Yetta's. "This is only our second date. I'm not ready to meet your whole family."

"Come on, everyone will be waiting to meet you," he said as he took Lily's hand, leading her off like a lamb to sacrifice. "What's the difference if you meet them now or later? It just happens that the yearly get-together is this weekend. My cousins are great. They'll love you," Philip soothed.

"What about your mother and aunts?"

"Did you forget? It was my mother who engineered our meeting."

Aunt Yetta's house was a white, rambling, two-story affair with a wrap-around porch that stood firmly against the sands of the New Jersey shoreline. Children chased each other in the front yard while sounds of adult laughter echoed from the rear. Lily tugged nervously at her shorts as she exited Philip's 1953 Oldsmobile. Aunt Yetta herself greeted them by the front steps, then stopped dead in her tracks.

"Philipka," she said in heavily Russian-accented English, never taking her eyes from Lily•in her white shorts. "Come, you're just in time to move the big table outside for lunch." She turned with a nod in Lily's direction. "And what do we have here?"

Five aproned women stepped through the screen door with military precision, lining the porch like soldiers on review. The sisters were all tall, generous in girth. All wore snow-white hair in a variety of short styles. One, younger than the rest, walked across the lawn towards the sidewalk.

"My dear Philipka, how nice," she said. "You've brought a young lady to us this afternoon." In a nimble gesture, Sadie Bogdonoff embraced her son and extended a dimpled hand to Lily.

"Welcome, welcome. And does this young person have a name?"

"Sorry, Mom. This is Lily Bloom. You met her mother at Mr. Katz's last fall."

"Ah, yes. And how is your mother? I haven't seen her since we got acquainted that time by the butcher. Is your father any better? I remember distinctly he wasn't well. Am I right?"

"Yes. It's kind of you to inquire," Lily answered politely, taking the well-manicured hand. "He has a bad heart and hasn't been able to work for some time. Ma caters for the synagogue, so she often goes to Fourth Street for kosher meat."

"Well, come in. We are preparing a snack for the young ones before they take a dip. Join me and my sisters in the kitchen while Philip moves the extra table with the men."

Sadie steered Lily firmly by the elbow through the lineup of aunts into an aroma-filled kitchen that faced the beach. Philip followed, separated from Lily by the six well-upholstered women.

"Run along, Philip," Sadie said. "Moishe is by the garage. Lily is safe with us, don't worry."

As Aunt Yetta shoed Philip out the back door, Sadie turned to Lily. "These are my sisters. Yetta, you already met. This is Rosa, Gertie, Sylvia and Eva. Like the Gabor sisters we are," she added.

"Philip told me about his aunts," Lily said, surrounded by the women in the increasingly cramped kitchen. "I'm glad to meet everyone. In my family, we have four girls."

"So you're from Parkside in Camden, I heard," said Eva. "Is that a Jewish neighborhood? Isn't some goyishka reform temple near there?" She had hardly given Lily a chance to reply before Sylvia, aunt No. 3, took up the interrogation.

"What kind of business is your father in? Are you related to the Blooms from dry goods on the White Horse Pike?"

"Your mother works?" asked Sadie, with a censorious shake of her head. "How does she have time for you and your little sister, with the housework and all?"

The sisters concluded their inquest with a resounding "vey." What more was there to ask? In 1954, a working mother was an anomaly, leaving no doubt as to the financial state of a family.

Peppered with questions, Lily was retreating to the screened porch when she felt a male presence behind her.

"Enough already, Tante," said a deep bass voice. "You're making the poor girl faint." An unseen man with strong hands suddenly spun Lily around. With a gasp she looked up to a 6-foot-6, black-mustachioed giant grinning down at her.

"Hello, I'm Alex, Tante Yetta's youngest. And you are?"

"I'm Lily Bloom from Camden, Philip's girlfriend."

"Well, well. Philip has very good taste. Where did he find such a beauty?"

His black eyes peered mischievously from under a thatch of dark hair. Alex had high cheekbones and a deeply cleft chin. Unlike his cousin, there was no winsome space between his perfectly spaced front teeth sparkling from his tanned face.

"Actually, in a butcher shop. I mean our mothers..." Lily hesitated.

"So it's a shiddach then. In America, that doesn't count. Come out with me on Friday night, Lily Bloom. I know how to show a girl a good time, not bring her to a boring cousin's club meeting. What was Philip thinking with a beauty like you? He knows how partial I am to tiny women."

Philip magically reappeared. "I see you've met my rogue cousin, Alex. Don't believe a word he says. He lies to women all the time. Go, Alex, get the chairs from the garage. I came to rescue Lily from the battleships."

"I've already done that. You should be more careful, leaving Lily alone when I'm around." Alex responded with a piercing glance in Lily's direction.

"So, you got acquainted with my dangerous cousin Alex and the girls." Philip said, shooting a venomous glance at the departing Alex. "Let's head for the beach."

"I couldn't get in one word between your mother and the aunts. Why didn't you warn me I'd get the third degree? What am I doing here today? How can you bring a girl to meet your family on the second date? "

"Now is as good a time as any since I plan to marry you after graduation next year."

"You're crazy. I'm not marrying anyone next year. In fact, you can take me home right now."

"Don't be silly. It's a glorious Sunday and besides, we just got here. My aunts slaved all morning over the perogi and stuffed cabbage. Eat something, at least. Anyway, I was saving the marriage proposal for the next date. But there it is. I'm marrying you next year."

"Quit saying that," protested Lily, pushing with both hands against Philip's chest. But a barely perceptible smile played at the corners of her mouth.

"Come on, Lily, let's get some fresh air. We can cool off by the water. Do you feel like going in? You can change into your bathing suit upstairs if you want."

"Not on your life. Don't look now, but I can feel your mother and aunts peeping out the kitchen window critiquing my shorts."

"They're a hundred years old and just plain jealous of how fine you look in those shorts. When we're married you can wear them every day. In fact, you can alternate with the red dress from last week."

Lily burst out laughing. The June sky was cerulean blue overhead. The water lapped at their bare feet as they made their way across the fine white sand holding hands. They were perfect in their youth, happy and certain about the future.

***

A resonant bass responded when I answered the phone on Monday afternoon. I knew immediately it wasn't Philip Bogdonoff.

"Who is this? Alex? Yes, I'll see if she's home yet," I lied.

Lily appeared from the kitchen, a quizzical expression on her face. "Who's Alex?" I whispered as I handed her the receiver. I remained close.

Lily did not mince words. "How did you get my number, Alex?" she demanded. "Easy to find Blooms in Camden, eh? You are a slippery character, especially since Phil is your cousin. No, we've only gone out twice. Well, no. I'm not seeing anyone steady but I need to think about this. Call me back after dinner," Lily stalled. "I...all right then. Friday evening it is. Seven? Fine."

She put the phone down and gave me a resigned look.

"I just made a date with Philip's cousin, Alex. What am I doing, Iris? Alex is a handsome hunk but the total opposite of Philip. He's got that 'bad boy' aura, definitely part of his charm."

"You know how Dad can size up that type in five seconds," I cautioned. "You may be in for a serious embarrassment."

Alex was late Friday evening. Lily fidgeted upstairs while Dad and I sat downstairs waiting for the doorbell. Dad had already voiced his concern about Alex. After all, what kind of lowlife moves in on his cousin's girl?

Just as I brought Dad a cup of tea from the kitchen, the bell rang.

"Get the door, Irisel. How does a man keep a girl waiting forty minutes on a first date?" Dad fumed, sotto voce.

"Hello, cutie pie. You must be the little sister," Alex said, filling the room with his enormous presence.

"Good evening, sir." He turned to my father. "I'm Alex Verasov. Is Lily ready?"

Dad inclined his head in my direction while at the same time signaling for Alex to take a seat. Despite Alex's size and Dad's frailness, no stranger was getting out the door with his daughter without a few questions. Even I knew the drill.

"So, Lily tells me you are from South Philly. What line of work are you in?" Dad began.

"After the service, I went into our haberdashery store, Kicks and Lids, on Snyder Avenue," Alex responded smoothly. "Ever hear of it?"

Dad ignored the question. "So, you didn't take advantage of the G.I. Bill for college?"

"What for? I grew up in the business. That's all I know."

"Shame," Dad countered. "Education is a gift. A grateful nation offered our vets a free ride to school after World War II. It was a great opportunity."

From upstairs, Lily began her descent for her "wow" entrance as Alex and Dad both rose from their chairs. Watching Alex intently, Dad offered his hand to the younger man. Alex never saw the outstretched hand. He was leering openly at Lily's carefully waxed legs, then Lily herself in the red silk dress.

Dad's expression darkened. Suddenly, there was a loud *slap*.

"You think I was born yesterday? I can't see what's on your mind? Get the hell out of here, you mamzer. Not now, not ever will you take out my daughter," Dad yelled at the top of his lungs, and he sank back into the wingchair, exhausted.

Lily ran and knelt by Dad, not exactly sure what had transpired. Dad's expression was like death, his breathing labored. Alex had his palm to his cheek, in shock from the blow.

"I'm sorry, Alex. You have to go. Ma's out and Dad's not well."

"Not well? He hauled off on me and he's not well?" Alex retorted. "I'm leaving. If this is the way you treat a guy, Philip can have you."

"Out," Dad sputtered as I ran for his nitro.

And just like that, the path cleared for Philip Bogdonoff.

***

Dad was failing. Doctors, oxygen tanks, EMS people all crowded the house at intervals, trying to wrestle him from death's grip while he grew paler and paler, sinking into his dying heart. Lily had graduated from high school early in June. Her marriage to Philip, scheduled for the last week of the month, had to be held at the house because Dad could not be moved. It was a bittersweet time.

"Lily, you'll send Philip by Mr. Katz's this morning on his way over from Philly," Ma said in a distracted voice. "I'm making the chopped liver for tomorrow, and I'll need my meat order." Can you blame her? Catering a wedding with a dying husband was no mean trick. She had gone into overdrive for Lily and Philip's reception, up with Dad's cries for morphine in the night, organizing the house by day, arranging the flowers and cooking. She was a tower of strength.

"Irisel, peel these potatoes for the kugels and shell the walnuts. Your sister is coming early this morning to help me with the jello molds and pastries. Wait, run upstairs to Dad before you start to make sure he doesn't need anything."

"Yes, Ma," I said, understanding this was no time to tell her I was supposed to go to a friend's to play that morning. I knew about responsibility. I was "up to the big ages," like Ma used to say. Ten years old.

The afternoon of Lily's wedding, Dad sat in his pajamas and robe in the wingchair, too weak to dress for the ceremony. An intimate group of family and friends gathered in the living room awaiting the rabbi's arrival. Upstairs, I helped Lily zip the delicate, white lace sheath she had chosen for the simple ceremony.

"So, what do you think?" she asked, perching the satin cap with tulle trim in her hair, then fastening Ma's pearls around her throat.

"You look like a bride should look—gorgeous," I said, exhaling. "You really do, and the hat is just enough, like Ma said."

Hugging my sister, I ran downstairs to join the well-wishers. I stationed myself on the ottoman close to Dad just as the first bars of "Oh Promise Me" sounded from the Victrola.

Lily and Philip, the rabbi, Philip's parents and Ma gathered under the chupah, the marriage canopy. When the rabbi placed the glass under Philip's foot at the end of the ceremony to symbolize the destruction of the Temple in Jerusalem, I looked into my father's face. All the pain of his illness, all the vulnerability of a lifetime was etched there. For the first time ever, I saw tears streaming down Dad's cheeks as he whispered in my ear, "Forgive me, my sweetheart. I won't be there for you on your wedding day. I won't live to crow over my grandchildren. But remember me, remember the love." His shoulders shook as he held me tightly against his chest.

***

That moment returned with a rush the day of my wedding. As I sat alone waiting for Ma to help me with my veil, I felt his presence like an unseen breath. His arms encircled me once again, his heartbeat and mine echoing a world of sorrow and love. I wept in silence for the sparkling future he would never see, the babies he would never hold. First on Lily's wedding day, then on mine, and even half a century later on my golden wedding anniversary, I remember the words of my father. How could I ever forget?

Where the Wild Things Are

by Sierra Mendez

Editor's Note: The last names of Ethan and his parents have been omitted because Ethan is a minor.

The horses were René's idea. She has two of them—a giant, sweet-tempered Gypsy Vanner called Xena who works with autistic children and a stocky, 14-hand pest named Jay-Jay who bears almost exclusive responsibility for the number of broken fences at his barn. René has used horse therapy with many of the compromised children she works with and has seen the good it brings.

René spent one fall convincing Ethan's mother, Annette, to let him visit the barn and meet the horses. They talked about possible germs, uneven ground, ill-behaved mares, raucous dogs, blood-sucking insects, manure and wayward tractor equipment. René brought pictures of her horses to Ethan and his mom, wore her cowboy boots into the apartment without wiping them on the mat, and talked about the magical place that was Esperanza Farms. Finally, Annette agreed to allow René to take Ethan to meet the horses with the understanding that she was not expected to accompany them; Annette hates dogs.

Esperanza Farms is located on the northeast outskirts of San Antonio, Texas, in the hills of a small town called Helotes and less than a mile from the famous Flores Country Store. A long, white fence leads up the gray drive, past oak trees and weeds and grass and flowers. There's an old water tower where the drive forks at the overgrown remains of a vegetable garden. The space is full of noises—the swish of dogs' tails and the scratch of cats' nails and the efficient click of boots.

Take a right at the fork and there's a sprawling house with five dog beds on the front porch, a make-shift volleyball court and a garden of blue plumbago, red salvia, and Esperanza. Take a left at the fork and there's a long swinging gate, a green storage unit overflowing with tools and a mesquite tree wilting in the Texas heat. The gravel drive loops around a sandy pen with a tall fence and towards a white barn with an old wooden floor worn by decades of sun and rain and pounding hooves.

***

Half an hour away, on a scrubby piece of land in the middle of San Antonio, close to Lackland Air Force Base and off of Loop 410, sits a gray strip of gravel called Horal Street. It's a narrow road, bumpy from decades of repair, with a skinny sidewalk on one side that begins and ends sporadically. Nearby highway signs flash in orange: "Limit Outdoor Activity: Air Pollution Levels High." The air is thick with the cackling of black grackle-birds nesting on telephone lines and bushes.

Halfway down this street is an apartment complex with tannish walls and greenish shutters. In Building C of the complex, up stairs of cement and iron, is a door with a scratchy Welcome Home mat and brass letters. Maroon plaques warn "No Smoking" and "No Animals." It's quieter here in the dark breezeway of the door where the concrete is stained with spilt coffee and half smoked cigarettes.

On the other side of the front door are textured white walls, small furniture and four table chairs. The kitchen is almost microscopic—something that belongs in the efficiency of a co-ed subsisting on microwavable pizzas and turkey sandwiches. There's no art on the walls, and the dark curtains stay closed. All focus seems to be on the large, high-definition TV that, with its size and clarity, has the ability to transport its viewers to another place. The carpet is a landmine strewn with toys.

A boy lives here, behind these closed doors and closed curtains, staring at what little light filters through. Out of the boy's mouth tumbles mumbling and grunting noises as he scoots and crawls his way around these rooms, his hair as black and soft as the grackle-bird's wings. His body is small and strong, and his eyes are dark in the delicate skin of his face, glowing in the apartment's pale luminous light like a fish in a watery cave.

Ethan is 7 years old. He's lived in this apartment his whole life where ten nurses and teachers and doctors and therapists keep vigil over him, testing his blood, his eyes, his heart, his lungs, his ears and his mind. He's 7 years old, and he only steps outside every other weekend when he is transported to another room in another apartment. Ethan is 7 years old and has never spoken a word. Nor has he ever seen anything that was not within six inches of his face. He has metal devices in his ears like steel antennas and cannot swallow without aspirating. He'll need heart surgery soon.

Ethan has Charge syndrome; his mother and doctors never expected him to make it this long.

Ethan was diagnosed with Charge syndrome when he was an infant. He has holes in his eyes and sees the world as though looking through a slice of Swiss cheese and a grimy, fogged window. His weakened lungs make even a minor allergy or cold a major threat that can send him to the hospital. His stunted heart prevents enough blood from reaching his organs to support his motions and movements. He can't hear except in bursts, even with the aid of medical devices that enhance vibrations to his eardrums.

Medical experts consider Charge syndrome one of the most complex conditions affecting children and adults. Caused by a minor mutation of the Chromosome CHD7 gene, it impairs—and sometimes destroys—the functions of the body's major organs like the heart and lungs, short-circuiting the development of the eyes, ear, nose, throat and genitalia. It is a birth defect that occurs in one of every nine to ten thousand births. His mom says that when Ethan was born, his doctors suggested putting him in a home or institution.

René Laminack is Ethan's teacher. She's worked with him four times a week for three hours each time for ten months. René has worked with children with disabilities in both public schools and private homes for 12 years, and for years before that with troubled teens. Currently, René works with seven compromised children and their families. She says Ethan is very different from them.

According to the Charge Syndrome Foundation website, doctors who work closely with Charge syndrome patients and are now beginning to realize it doesn't always affect their minds, only their bodies. René says Ethan is different from her other students because he *knows* something is wrong.

Today is one of Ethan's bad days. He wanted Cheerios for breakfast and got mushed-up ham instead. His nurse says he got mad and threw the mush at her. He tried to play with his blocks but they—his caretakers—kept coming in, poking and prodding and taking his temperature and making him stand and making him sit and pointing to the signs on the walls. His nurse can cite the dozens of times Ethan has torn down these signs labeling rooms and items in the house if forced to look at them for too long.

René brought the box with the colors and sounds today. She says they had fun, but then she tried to show him that thing with her hands that he can barely see and the sounds he can barely hear, and she says he got frustrated. René thinks it angers Ethan that he doesn't know what she's trying to tell him.

Ethan has been taught how to move his hands to tell someone he doesn't want something, so he does it again and again. He signs, "no, no, no." And other caretakers keep coming. With their scratchy clothes and hard, cold things. René says Ethan hates being touched with their scratchy clothes and hard, cold things and hands that don't seem to care that he hates it. He signs, "no, no, no."

René thinks that, for Ethan, all of those people crowding around all of the time make the air feel tight and scary. They press in on him from all sides. They speak in hushed voices. In response, Ethan's hands flutter to his chest and stay there. He curls up into a small ball, hiding himself from what he doesn't like and what scares him.

His doctors make him swallow those things again and again and again. One of Ethan's nurses, Karen, says it makes him act differently because it makes his head feel fuzzy and his blood pump too hard and makes him feel angry. So he throws his toys at René. Ethan tries to tell them what he wants with noises and grunts and his hands. He signs, "no, no, no." But no one ever seems to get it, and it makes him madder.

He tries to show them what he wants. Karen says he's trying to make his eyes work when he pulls at them and sometimes when bangs his head against the table. René and his doctor say that sometimes he can make them work. Today he can't. Karen notes that his legs won't work today. She says sometimes he can make them work. Today he can't. He's angry he *can't*. No matter how hard he tries or how hard he fights or what he does, today he can't make things happen. He signs, "no, no, no."

Annette wants Ethan well. She can't count the hours she's spent in the hospital waiting for his next breath, counting his seconds. She can't count the money she's spent on doctors, nurses, toys, therapists, speech teachers, pills and medicines to keep Ethan well. Her apartment is sparse with things that are hers—basic kitchen table, small couch, two small mirrors, some art made out of brightly colored cut cloth. Ethan's room, on the other hand, is a menagerie of blue and cars and bright toys—a world to keep her son safe. She's not sure what she'll do when Ethan grows too big for his world. Maybe little boys are like goldfish—if you keep their bowls small enough, they'll never be too big to live safely inside them. Ethan makes it so hard sometimes. Every minute is a struggle, every second a demand or a need. And Ethan is not an affectionate child. He's tough and wiry and slippery when she tries to hold him.

Annette wants Ethan to learn sign language so that Ethan can talk to her like other kids can. She's frustrated that Ethan has learned only a handful of signs when "the experts say" he should have learned around 70 by now. She wishes she knew how to change him. She wishes she could tell Ethan what she wants and that he would kiss her without her asking. She wishes she could teach Ethan when he is bad and when he is good. She wishes Ethan could talk to other people to tell them what he needs. She wishes she could understand.

Karen is Ethan's other mom and Annette's former partner. As one of his nurses, Karen spends more time with Ethan than anyone else; and as an R.N., Karen is the decision maker regarding his physical needs. Karen wants Ethan to walk. She wants him to be active and independent. She wants him to be strong so he can do the things he wants to do and healthy so he can have new experiences. She hopes heart surgery will make him strong enough that he *can* do those things without the Viagra to make his lungs stronger and his heart pump better. She wants Ethan to have the chance to see things like other kids—like Disneyland, the zoo, and the Grand Canyon. She thinks that the apartment is too small and too comfortable. She thinks kids need more space.

She wonders what kind of life he's going to have.

René wants Ethan to be Ethan. She wants to introduce him to new environments and let him experience the world outside of his apartment in the unique ways he experiences things. She thinks that if she can do this, he'll change. She believes Ethan has considerable intelligence and energy, yet every day is the same for him—a day of never realizing his wishes. She thinks it's very frustrating for him and that's why he's angry all the time. René knows Ethan will never be like other children, but she's convinced he can still be happy, healthy and alive and that there are better ways to make him that way.

***

Today is Ethan's first trip to the barn. It is a warm day near the end of winter and Ethan is wearing his Buzz Lightyear shirt. He, René, and Karen stand by a white iron gate at the entrance to Esperanza Farms—dogs barking, grass crackling, afternoon air perfumed by the mountain laurel blooming on a nearby hillside, the smell as purple as grape Jolly Ranchers—while Ethan screams. A scream that writhes in the air and pierces the tallest tree branches, a scream that grunts and hiccoughs and squirms to get away.

René thinks it's the bigness. The strangeness. The pull of the trees and the emptiness of the sky and the missingness of a ceiling. It's the absence of walls and the goneness of windows and curtains. It's the weirdness of smells and the greatness of space and the unfamiliar brush of the moving and unknown. Ethan curls himself into a ball against Karen to avoid all of the something bads that can fit in that big emptiness.

Flailing and fighting against Karen's arms and legs, Ethan is walked from the gate to the picnic table. A Hawaiian print table cloth covers it, dogs run around it, and behind it sits a large pasture filled with grass and a herd of horses. Now alternating between screams and grunts, Ethan is helped to sit on the bench.

Then Ethan goes quiet. René says he's trying to know. Large things move to his left, different from the soft, fuzzy things under his feet. Different from the people pressing around him. These things are big. They move slowly and lazily, then with dashing jumps. There are lots of them close by. Ethan's black eyes are shiny and wide and glossy and turned towards them. The big things move closer, and Ethan's eyes get bigger. He has come to the place where the wild things are. They stomp their giant hooves and swish their giant tails. They toss their giant heads and kick their giant legs until Ethan stays very still and does his magic trick of listening to bodies move and tasting sounds and smells without blinking his eyes once. And the wild things notice this and accept him. And in their company, it seems like Ethan is no longer afraid.

Karen stands with her arms folded across her chest, sunglasses on. She leans away from the dogs when their tails wag against her and stays firmly on the road, away from the grass and manure and barn cats. She barely looks at the horses. Then she begins fluttering around the picnic table where Ethan sits, consoling and wringing and questioning and pointing. Encouraged by Ethan's quiet, worried by Karen's fear, and desperate for this trip to go well lest Ethan's moms decide he shouldn't venture out of the apartment again, René buzzes around trying to engage Ethan's interest. She doesn't want to introduce him to a horse yet; she has a feeling it will be too much for his mother. So René decides to focus on getting Ethan used to the space. She brings him horse brushes to touch and pushes grain into his hands. Karen sees this and thinks it is right and begins bringing hay and halters and leather girths and lead ropes to Ethan, as well.

With every item pressed and every thing presented, Ethan grows tenser. His head starts swiveling. His eyes grow wider. His hands start shaking. His back hunches as he rocks. He reaches for Karen, then squirms to get down. He signs, "No, no, no." René and Karen give up and sit down on the picnic table with Ethan, on either side of him, blocking what they think is so upsetting to him. Ethan continues to sign, "No, no, no."

Then the red-haired lady who owns the barn sets a small flower on the table next to Ethan. René and Karen immediately pick it up and press it into his palm. They want him to feel its soft petals, smell its sour freshness and see its bright color. Ethan flinches away and lets the flower fall to the ground, rocking backward again. The barn lady picks up the yellow bud and places it on the table next to Ethan again before walking away. She takes René and Karen with her to show them a very pregnant mare in a stall nearby.

Ethan grows still, neck tight, and shoulders watchful. His eyes move quickly, never focusing. His fingers move through the breeze, curious and questioning. His nose is raised slightly in the air,

nostrils flaring with the new smells. The big things move sleepily. The furry things run around him. Something small is next to his leg. Ethan's hand reaches towards the flower, seeking where it lay against the hard, grainy wood of the tabletop. He picks it up very gently, very slowly, and with no one looking, he twirls it luxuriously between his fingers.

The red-haired barn lady has a different plan than René and Karen. Without waiting for say-so, she fetches Raine from the pasture. Raine is a bay Arab mare, fine-boned and athletic. Her halter is blue. The red-haired lady doesn't lead Raine directly to Ethan but to the grassy patch beyond him. She lets the rope go slack so that Raine can graze.

But Raine doesn't want to graze. A small thing is sitting not far from her, still and quiet. Different from the tall things striding around and the quick, fuzzy things dodging between her legs. Raine's body stills, neck arches and ears perk, listening for movement and intent. Her eyes are moving, watchful. Her tail swishes in the breeze, curious and questioning. Her nose pushes forward through the air, nostrils flaring with the new scent.

The small thing doesn't move.

The red-haired barn lady, Janine Mendez, doesn't really know Ethan. She's known René for a long time, and she's known horses her whole life. But this is the first time she's met Ethan. Still, Janine does know children. She's had four of them herself and countless little ones visiting the barn to learn to ride, to run faster than the wind, to sit up tall and keep their hands gentle. She's taught them to brush and groom and take care of things that need them, to grow up and be responsible for another's life. They learn how much shorter animal's lives are than theirs and the pain and acceptance and unconditional love that must come with that knowledge.

Janine knows about things that need to be wild and need to be free. She knows that it must be accepted that things happen—that horses grow and children develop and animals die —in their own time, and they must be allowed that time. She knows it's all about what they're ready for. She knows you can't force anything.

She says that humans try to force everything. They rarely accept. There's always want, always more, always what's missing, always what-could-be-had and what-could-be-gotten. They're always thinking of Tomorrow, of Next, of In Ten Years, and they push and prod the present. They want tomorrow now. They want more now. They want next now. They never see the now that actually is, only the next that could be.

Janine knows that all children like Ethan have is now. She knows their world, unlike ours, is unavoidably shaped by their bodies, which roots them in the feeling and condition of the present. She knows the expectations and values placed on other children do not apply to them and yet, she says, we try to apply them because it's the only way we know how to be. But children like Ethan exist in their own time and act in their own time. They're lives are not "on the clock" and "on the tight schedule" that ours are. Janine says that's what creates the tension and the struggle—all these children have is now, and we're not capable of being there. Because we're not capable of accepting that. That's why Janine wants Ethan to meet Raine and the other horses and the dogs. Animals live in the now better than we do.

Ethan sits still as a stone on his perch on the picnic table. Head moves. Hands move. Cool breeze brushes skin with unfamiliar smell. Ethan inhales deeply, smelling. It's one of the big things.

Unfamiliar. Close.

Ethan shrinks back.

Clicks his tongue.

Hands flutter. Shoulders pull up and curl in.

Raine steps forward and lowers head, shoulders down, inhaling deeply. Eyes forward, ears forward, nose moving with the breeze and scent of boy.

Ethan moves his hands to his eyes. Pulls at the skin around them.

Raine moves forward and stills.

Ethan rocks forward and stills.

Raine inhales air, scent, muscles taut with alertness

Ethan inhales air, scent, muscles taut with alertness.

Raine sticks out tongue to taste boy's scent on the air, round and pink.

Ethan stares.

Raine sticks out tongue to taste boy's scent on the air, round and pink.

Ethan stills.

Raine takes a step closer and sticks out tongue to taste the boy's scent.

Ethan sticks out his tongue, round and pink.

***

Horses are herd animals. They spend their lives in groups, listening to one another's movements, talking to each other in ways alien to humans. Pinned ears are a threat. A raised tail means agitation or excitement. Pacing is distress. Horse's skin can shiver on command, a trick mostly used to dislodge flies.

Everyone at Esperanza Farms knows that Grace, Raine's daughter, is in love with another Arab at the barn named Gus. They are never apart, and Gus runs in circles around Grace whenever someone tries to catch her. Jenny and Sparkle are best friends, humorously because Sparkle is an 18-hand Quarter Horse mare and Jenny is an 11-hand pony. Lightning and Charlie have both passed away now, but they spent their thirties roaming Esperanza Farms together, sharing each other's food and each other's age.

Raine came to Esperanza in 1993 from Brighter Days Farm—a rescue stable for abused horses. Over the years, many of the horses at Esperanza have come from Brighter Days. There was Jezebel, a black-bay thoroughbred mare, who was wild and fast and wouldn't let her previous owners catch her. She was, therefore, deemed useless by them. There was Apple Jack, a spotted Appaloosa gelding neglected in a stall for years and covered with barn sores and infections from flies, his muscles weak from lack of movement. And there was Cooper, a black-bay thoroughbred terrified of people and anything that came near his head from the years he spent as a racehorse when a man with a whip hit him regularly on the face to make him run faster.

Raine was 2 in 1993. She'd been rescued from a man who had dozens of horses and no means to support them. They were all locked together in a small pen with limited food—all of the horses, from large, aggressive stallions to small, still-growing fillies. Raine was pregnant when she came to Esperanza, her ballerina frame heavy and back scarred from the stallions' violence. Janine had fallen in love with her on sight at Brighter Days and brought her home. She was too young and too delicate and too malnourished to support the baby. It was stillborn. It was buried by the water tank at the back of the property. Now Raine has another daughter, the half-Arab Paint named Grace.

Raine has always taken of the children who ride her like a bossy older sister. She quickly rose in the ranks of the herd to head mare and the formidable protector of young horses. Her daughter, as a baby, would prance through the herd like a princess while Raine followed behind with her ears pinned, daring the other horses to lay a hoof on Grace. And when another mare died from birthing complications, Raine adopted the baby filly and guarded over her as though she were her own.

In America, the use of horses for therapy began in the 1970s. It had been established as a formalized discipline only ten years before when it was used in Germany, Austria and Switzerland as an adjunct to traditional physical therapy. Scientifically, the success of hippotherapy is related to the rocking motion of the horse and the resulting movement of the rider, which stimulates spinal nerves directly connected to critical nerves in the brain.

This scientific description, however, does not explain all of the benefits of hippotherapy, particularly for children like Ethan who do not actually ride the horse due to their physical restrictions. There's something mystic about this part, something at odds with modern vaccines and plastic surgical equipment. Yet the effectiveness of horse therapy has been cited time and time again with far more consistency than other scientific experiments.

Ethan started trying to talk after one trip to the barn and his time with Raine. Other children who spend their time curled in a tiny ball in their wheelchairs have been introduced to a horse and spread their arms wide in welcome. Wounded Warriors, a group for veterans, uses horse therapy to help soldiers with PTSD. The North Texas area has more than two dozen centers for therapeutic riding, helping everyone from children with disabilities to troubled teens. Rupert Isaacson, a man from Austin, Texas, whose son has autism, witnessed remarkable changes in his son after three years of riding. He wrote a book called *The Horse Boy*, created a film documentary by the same name and started The Horse Boy Foundation to help make horses and nature available to other children, autistic or not, who might not otherwise have access to them.

"With the horses," René says, "I think it's the motion. And the warmth. And the kindness. They breathe in and they breathe us in. And they breathe out and we breathe out. And you realize that you're really the same."

With the horses, there's acceptance. Something no one else can really give Ethan, because, as humans, we worry too much. We're worried about his health and if something is going to make him sicker. We're worried about all those things he's never going to do or get to be. We're worried that he's not enough like us and if he'll always suffer for being different. We're worried about what he's thinking and what he's feeling and if he's going to die and if we're doing the right thing and what Ethan thinks of us. We're worried about what we did wrong or what we could do better.

And Ethan—a child who understands the world through feeling and sensing in a way that exists beyond sight and sound—feels that worry. And feels afraid because the people around him feel afraid. But the horse just breathes. And there is peace. And there is acceptance. And there is now. And there's nothing beyond that to worry about.

***

Today is Ethan's third trip to the barn. He sits on the picnic table, swinging his legs. Raine continues to eat, lips drawing up grain, flat teeth chewing musingly. Her neck is soft and warm in the 3 o'clock sun, and her eyes close lazily. Ethan's whole body strains both towards Raine and away. His arms are clenched, his weight rocking. His face is set on the horse's face, eyes directed towards it but never focusing. His hands move towards his eyes; his fingers spread—thumbs on his cheekbones, fingers on his forehead. They pull at the delicate skin around his eyes, black irises as wide and as glossy as marbles. Ethan's face is baby doll smooth and pale. He rocks forward and back and forward. His hands jerk back to his chest, backs of his fingers pressed against his blue shirt. He rocks forward and forward.

Raine moves closer.

Ethan's mouth opens partially. Small, liquid sounds come streaming out. Then stop. Stream out. Then stop.

Raine moves closer.

Ethan's shoulders twitch, hands flutter. Nose flares with familiar smell. Soft noises come from Ethan's mouth, bird noises. Coos.

Raine moves closer still, mouth no longer moving with food. Neck soft, ears forward, eyes soft, nose inquiring. Movements are slow, measuring.

Ethan's legs swing from side to side and back and forth and side to back to forth. Familiar. Sharp outtake of air in delight, in laughter.

Raine's nose lowers and nudges boy's shoulder. Rests there.

Ethan's body stills. Coos.

Ethan's language is the language of crickets and frogs, of tails swishing in the darkness, of ears erect and on guard. Ethan's language is that of the first humans—the language of gestures where a thousand distinct messages could be conveyed in the delicate wrists and the fluttering of fingers, in the movement of shoulders and the posture of necks, in the direction of a chin and the lift of a nose. Ethan's language is of the body and the senses.

Our language is of the mind and its conceptions. While Ethan's is a statement of what *is,* ours is a statement of what we *think* it is. It is our concession to one another. Some of the most important people in Ethan's life are desperate for him to learn sign language. René does not think, however, that this is so that they can better understand his needs. She thinks it's so that he can better understand theirs and become more like them.

René cites speech pathologists who have worked with Ethan and who have told these important people that sign language is not the most useful solution for him. They say it would be better for him to try alternative methods more aligned with his physical capabilities; Karen herself says she and Ethan spend so much time together she can read his language even though it's not hers.

Annette, however, insists that he learn it. Ethan's doctor says it's important because it's "not possible to determine the child's cognitive ability" before a viable system of communication is established. When Karen was asked why Annette thinks it's important for Ethan to learn sign language, even though other ways work better and are more natural for him, she said it was so that he could talk to everyone and so he wouldn't be so different.

Dr. Linda Ward, an audiologist in the Speech and Hearing Sciences Department at the University of North Texas, explained the experiences of some parents with children like Ethan is akin to the grieving process—except that instead of one death, there are hundreds, and they happen in small ways every day. She says that every day is a struggle as parents realize the ways they can't help their child and begin to fear every decision is a mistake. She says most of these parents are looking for the chance for absolution.

Annette will never have that chance if Ethan cannot learn to understand her. If she cannot make him see that all her wringing, all her pulling, all her holding, all her fluttering, all her touching, all her pushing are the million ways she's signing "I'm sorry."

"I'm sorry, I'm sorry, I'm sorry, I'm sorry."

***

René says today is an exploring day. It's only Ethan and René, and she's not trying to show him those hand things anymore. Ethan smiles and laughs. Today is a slide day. Today he gets to put the ball on the slide, and today he's strong and he can pull it back, and today he can let it go, and the ball jumps high and hits the wall and there's a loud sound. Ethan does it over and over and over again. René says he likes to make things happen. He likes to see what happens when he does things.

He's been taught how to move his hands to say he likes something and wants it to keep happening. He signs, "More, more, more." Today is a talking box day. It's different from the other one. It's small, and he can make it do things. He can press this and a sound happens, this and a vibration happens, this and the color changes and Teacher will help him see it. He tries to put it in his mouth so that he can know it better, but René won't let him.

René says today is an experiment day. Today he can put his feet on things and move them around and feel them and learn about them. Today he can put his head on things and hear the tiny lines and waves they make and learn about them. Today is a standing day. Today Ethan figured out how to stand by himself. He scooted to the corner of the living room, tight into the corner. He braced one side of his body against the right corner and pushed and slid up. He braced the other side of his body against the left corner and pushed and slid up.

He signs, "More, more, more, more, more, more, more." It made René so happy.

Today is a talking day. "Nananananananananananananana. nananananananananananananana." Ethan sings it now, and René sings it with him.

Today Ethan can do things. Today he can make things happen.

***

Ethan's third trip to the barn was his last. René is resigning as his teacher because she refuses to teach him sign language, and Ethan's next teacher has no interest in horse therapy. Ethan will never see Raine, the dogs, the other horses and the barn again.

On the day at the barn that would be his last, Ethan was guided away from Raine and the picnic table by Karen and her friend, his head wobbling frantically up and down and side to side as he was lifted from the bench. His arms had become tense again. His body had seized again. His fingers on both hands had curled around his thumbs as though he was picking something up and began tapping together. Karen and her friend helped Ethan become steady on his feet. Out of sun and down the gray driveway, they'd shuffled back to car, Ethan's hands still pushing together insistently. René explained that he was signing "More."

"More, more, more, more, more."

> —*In memory of Maurice Sendick, who knew about little boys who need to be wild and need to be free and about a mother's wild love.*

The Girl Who Walked Across Fire

by Moira Muldoon

The coals are crunchy. They have been burning for hours, are fresh and hot—somewhere in the neighborhood of 1200 degrees Fahrenheit. The people lining up to walk across them are barefoot, jeans rolled up so a fraying hem string doesn't catch and light legs up. They have been told to walk. Running leads to tripping, they are told, and no one wants a burned face. I'm not sure why faces will burn but bare feet won't, but this is what we are told. To take off shoes, roll up our pants, look up. To say "Cool Moss" as a mantra. And then to walk calmly, powerfully, straight into the fire.

***

The concrete floor is actually shaking. At the Meadowlands Exposition Center in New Jersey just outside New York City, people are jumping up and down, dancing. It's 3 p.m. or 10 p.m. or 1 a.m. or all of the above—time is distorted when self-help guru Tony Robbins is exhorting us to celebrate. He waves his hands, his grin bright as any stage light. It's irresistible, and as it turns out, resisting is so little fun anyway.

I am here with my family: my younger brother, his wife, my mother, and a pair of my brother's friends I have long known and liked. Of the six of us, only my brother has firewalked before. He and my father had gone together when my brother was 12. I'd been invited, but declined because it conflicted with a school dance. And I'm pretty sure I thought it sounded weird.

It's a funny thing. My brother has been very successful. He's risen through the corporate ranks and is funny and thoughtful and easy to be around. For years, he's credited the firewalk with much of who he is, and I've wondered how much it really had to do with that success. When he called and asked if I wanted to go to "Unleash the Power Within," the firewalking seminar, I said yes without hesitation; it was a visceral response. For years, I had regretted not going the first time. My father had long since died, but my brother was offering another chance to answer a question that had lurked in the corners of my mind: What does it mean if, when you are 12, you learn that you can walk across fire? What could it have meant for me? Who could I be if I learned I could walk across fire?

***

"If the Saint calls you, if you have an open road, then you don't feel the fire as if it were your enemy," says a Greek villager in anthropologist Loring Danforth's book, *Firewalking and Religious Healing*. In northern Greece, he writes, people firewalk as part of a celebration of St. Constantine and St. Helen. Their unburned feet are signs. The villager says, "When I go into the fire, someone else is leading me—the Saint."

In the U.S., firewalking has been used by self-help gurus to promote self-confidence and the ability to change. It's about self-transformation—an idea nearly sacrosanct in the land of the American dream—and belief in the power of the individual.

Most people are bedeviled by the firewalk, how it works or whether it is an elaborate hoax. David Willey, a physics instructor at the University of Pittsburgh, and some of his friends set the world record for the world's hottest firewalk in 1997 in Edmond, Washington. He recorded the trench was 3.5 meters long and temperatures ranged from 1602 to 1813 degrees F. Only one man walked it at its hottest. Willey's theory, according to his web site, is that "the foot absorbs relatively little heat from the embers that are cooled, because they are poor conductors, that do not have much internal energy to transmit as heat, and further that the layer of cooled charcoal between the foot and the rest of the hot embers insulates them from the coal's [sic]."

Mythbusters—a popular and good-humored TV show dedicated to using science to prove or bust myths and urban legends—took on firewalking. The Mythbusters concluded that the "secret" was just knowing how to walk: Use a regular, steady pace so that you don't dig your heels in too deeply.

Other theories posit that the coals just aren't that hot. But according to a *National Geographic* interview with firewalking expert Tolly Burkan, people have heated metal grills and walked across them unharmed.

The truth as best I can tell is no one knows why it works. There are records of people getting burned—Robbins says he burned himself once and other people have been burned, too. But mostly, it seems that people from all different parts of the world and all different faiths and all parts of history walk safely through the fire.

***

When the seminar opens, a bunch of healthy, positive-looking folks in suits get up on stage, dancing to loud, pulsing music, clapping their hands in rhythm, some awkwardly. The lights glare and flash like the start of a rock concert. Production values are astounding—the sound board is enormous, manned by technicians who could as easily be working for a rock star. As the lights flare and the music thumps, I turn to my brother. "Just like a sales conference," he says.

Seriously? I'd never been to a sales conference. Then again, I wasn't a muckety-muck marketing executive.

"Yeah. This is exactly how they all start out. Getting everyone all pumped up. They're just not usually this big, with this many people." There are about 5,000 people at this seminar. My brother and his wife—also a marketing executive—start making jokes about conferences.

Not long after, Robbins himself comes out. He is a tall man, powerful and straight at 6-foot-7, but not particularly attractive. His features are a little out of proportion, as though different parts of his body grew asynchronously. His hands are enormous. Years ago, when my dad and brother firewalked, Robbins shook the hand of every person who did it. There were 100 or so then instead of today's roughly 5,000—and my brother came home talking not about the fire so much as about Robbins' enormous hands.

I had seen Tony Robbins in the movie *Shallow Hal* and thought he was flat and uninteresting. Watching him on stage, I realize that film is the wrong medium for him. Film can't capture his raw energy the way he captures and holds a crowd. There are people who come to life on stage in a way that's impossible to capture in any kind of recording. A Superchunk album is nothing to a Superchunk show. The same is true for the Old 97s, Bruce Springsteen and countless bands. The give and take between audience and performer is impossible to recreate in 2D. The handful of videos of Robbins live in a seminar are better, the way live albums are better. But still…

Robbins grins as soon as he gets to the front of the stage and in that moment, even before he begins speaking, he is magnetic. Electric. He swings his arms into a raised clap, and smiles, joyous as Christmas. In that instant, he owns the room. Owns it. It happens that fast, unlike anything I've ever seen. His smile is engaging, warm. His body is relaxed. His delight is palpable. And the energy in the room spirals upward.

Still, it happens so fast that I am skeptical. I find it worrisome when someone can walk on stage and in a matter of seconds own a room. It's worrisome when rock stars do it—much less someone who is going to tell you how to live your life.

Onstage, Robbins talks. And talks. And talks. For something like 12 hours. In some ways, what he says is little more than a series of clichés: Don't see things as better or worse than they are; see them *as* they are. Or: The story you tell yourself about yourself influences you; pick the story that empowers you. There are new twists on familiar topics, too: Energy is a habit; the more you move, the more you feel. Reasonable stuff.

There are parts that are just flat-out awful: gender stereotypes and strange, long and embarrassing interventions with people who say they have depression. Robbins doesn't believe much in depression, or more specifically, in anti-depressants. Which strikes me as nuts. At one point, men yell like Mel Gibson in *Braveheart* and women cry; one says she feels protected. My inner feminist shakes her head exhaustedly. My outer one, too.

Still, there are useful parts of the seminar. The thing that strikes me most and that stays with me is this: Early on in the seminar, Robbins asked us to write down what we prioritized in our lives and what we wanted our priorities to be. The choices were certainty, uncertainty, significance, love/connection, growth and contribution. My priority was certainty. When it came time to write down what we wanted our priorities to be, twice I wrote "uncertainty." Twice I crossed it out.

The quality of your life is directly proportional to the amount of uncertainty you can comfortably live with, Robbins said at the end of the exercise. Three months later, this is the line that's stayed with me the most.

For the four years before going to the seminar, my life had been a compendium of uncertainties, and I hadn't done well with it. My husband had gone to medical school as a 40-year-old, just a year after we'd gotten married and mere months after our first (intensely colicky) child was born. I'd switched from being an adjunct English professor at a big state university to a freelance corporate writer in order to support us. We'd changed cities. The whole thing was rough.

By the time I got to the Robbins seminar, my husband was a third-year med student, and we had two little kids who both slept through the night. I was done being pregnant and nursing, and my business was stable. Three weeks before the seminar, I had made the final payment on the credit card debt we'd gotten into during my husband's first year of school. In other words, I was more OK than I'd been in a long time. I was beginning to have the intellectual and emotional space to think about sane ways to live with uncertainty. Or, at the very least, to admit that resisting uncertainty didn't do any good.

***

Robbins grows stronger and more energetic as the day progresses, charging the crowd and the crowd charging him in an endless upward loop. He keeps us on our feet most of the day. "Celebrate!" he yells, when it seems the crowd is dimming a little, and the music picks up. It is execrable music—pop tunes and Enya and power ballads and the Celine Dion *Titanic* song. But then Robbins claps, an enormously resonant motion, and jumps up and down, his face lit with delight. People around us jump up and down with him and dance. I have never seen anything like this. And I want it: this whole body letting go. I jump up and down, throw my arms into the air, dance until I am sure my body will hurt. But it doesn't hurt.

As the night wears on, as we get closer and closer to the firewalk, he turns up the magnetism and charm. Robbins begins to talk about the actual act of walking the fire. "A guru taught me this mantra," he says. He draws a deep breath, uses his forefingers and thumbs to make two small circles in classic Indian style, and then chants: "M-I-C." Breath. "K-E-Y." Breath. "M-O-U-S-E." His timing is perfect. Everyone laughs.

By 10 p.m. we are actively getting ready for the firewalk. The rules are pretty straightforward: Make our moves (the gesture we'd trained our bodies to use to put us "in state" or in a good mental state); look up, rather than down at the coals; say "cool moss" (to crowd out negative thoughts); and walk straight, calmly, steadily.

Easy enough.

We go through a couple relaxation exercises that are meant to give us the equivalent of a couple of hours of sleep. Relax, relax. Then the energy is turned up again—more jumping, more music, more celebration. Robbins' voice is scratchy and warm and the place is alive with joy. It is exhilarating, and I feel great. Not crazy and pumped, but focused. Awake. Alive. I feel as good as I've ever felt. Clear.

***

We stay close together, the six of us, filing out of the expo center and down to the parking garage, where the trenches have been set up. Firemen and paramedics are everywhere. As we enter the garage I catch the eye of a fireman. He is maybe 25 and has really bad teeth. His hair is slicked back and he looks New York tough. He holds my gaze for a moment, then dips his head and shakes it in disgust, like "What's the matter with you people?" It must be strange for him to see people paying money to walk into fire. All I can think is how much he is missing by being cynical.

The music in the parking garage is loud, a kind of African drum beat playing in an endless loop, or perhaps live drummers. Oprah is in a new partnership with Robbins, and her crew is filming the seminar. You can watch her firewalk on YouTube these days and see her surprise that she could do it.

Staffers dance while physically guiding us into place. Our descent to the fire is loud and crowded but orderly, well-rehearsed and meticulously planned. The absolute orderliness of it, even through the loud music and dancing, somehow underscores the seriousness of what we are about to do, the possibility that people could fall and get burned. That *I* could fall and get burned. I hold onto my brother's waistband as I had done the New Year's Eve we spent on Bourbon Street, when the crowds were so intense that I was lifted off my feet and moved forward pressed shoulder to shoulder with the people next to me.

We clap our hands in rhythm and say "yes" over and over. I dance as I clap—I, who barely danced in public at my wedding. We are a lot of people, and I am short. I can't see the trenches of hot coals, though I know they are there. I can smell the burning coals, like an outdoor fire pit in a backyard, that smoky smell that clings to clothes and the next morning evokes the glorious night you had. It is closing in on 1 a.m., and we have been going straight since registering at 10 a.m. Though it is dark, I still haven't seen the actual coals because of the people crowded around. I feel my first twinge of nerves—will I really walk across fire? My feet in the fire? Not being able to see the coals makes them scarier, even though I know what they will look like.

We had taken our shoes off in the expo center and the night is cold; the pavement feels gritty and cold under my feet. I turn to my sister-in-law and say something like "Holy shit! We're going to walk into fire. What the hell are we doing?"

I am freaked out. Not because I am worried about burning, exactly. So many people have done it before me and been just fine. My 12-year-old brother had done it, for heaven's sake. It is strange to think about crossing the coals the way it's strange to think about jumping from a high dive or hang gliding or pushing your body to do something that goes counter to all natural instincts. The physical reality freaks me out, but also, I suspect, the metaphysical. What does it mean if I do it? What will I now need to do?

We are pulled into a single file, our pants rolled up, our feet bare. My brother's friend is in front of me, my brother and sister-in-law behind. I put my hand on Ben, the drums going and going. My brother is behind me, the tallness of both men forming a strange cocoon. I get clearer and more focused and relaxed the closer I come to the front of the line. A stillness in the midst of the music settles in. And then I can see the coals. They burn orange and bright and warm. My friends in front of me start walking across. I somehow don't see them. All I see are the coals.

The staffers put me onto the grass at the beginning of the trench. It feels cool and soft on my feet even as the staffer's arms are hard and forceful in guiding me into the right place. They tell me to go, but I need to catch my breath, I need to think about what I need to do. Look up, look up, say "Cool Moss." The staffers say something in my ears, something I can't understand. They switch gears and begin chanting "yes" with me.

I don't remember deciding to walk. I don't remember taking the first step, whether the air felt warm on my soles. My first clear thought is that the coals are crunchy. That all I can feel is crunch. My second thought is that they are hot—and I should probably keep moving. I look up, up, and say nothing. No mantra, no "Cool Moss," no anything but moving, moving, moving across the coals.

And then I am at the end, and my feet are in cool grass soaked with water. It had been six steps or perhaps ten. Not many. I wipe my feet to get rid of any coals that might have stuck between my toes. I feel stinging on the instep of my foot, low and dull. I have been burned, though only a little. A few small blisters that will go away the next day. I am ecstatic. It is unlike anything I have ever felt, a deep stillness in me in the midst of the noise and also absolute thrilling delight. My brother's friend hugs me in the most enormous bear hug possible and my sister-in-law flies into my brother's arms, her whole body wrapped around him. I would burst into tears if I wasn't so busy hollering at the top of my lungs.

***

The sheer delight and energy stay with me for weeks. Though I'd come to the seminar to do a thing I'd always wished I had, it turns out that what I really wanted was just to let go. Yes, I wanted to be better and yes, I wanted my life to be bigger, but mostly, I'd been wound tight for a long time. Throughout the whole first day, the hours of Robbins talking and the flashing lights and swelling music, the image that had played in my mind over and over was of my fist, turning palm up and opening. I wanted to drink the Kool-Aid. I wanted to dance with strangers. I wanted to throw myself under a showman's spell for a day. And I wanted to do it in safety—with people I loved around me, in a place that was familiar to me from my family's own mythologies.

The actual firewalk itself was a blast—I'd walk across coals again in a heartbeat. I'd do it once a week if there was time and somebody to build me a proper trench. It's fascinating and crazy good fun, like roller coasters or bodysurfing big waves. But the real thrill for me was in giving myself over just for a day to the swell and the pulse of emotions rising upward, higher and higher. So much joy. So much excitement. So much delight. I was buoyant.

Robbins says the firewalk is just a metaphor. It's to show us how much more we can do than we think. He uses the firewalk as a starting point to help people transform their lives. The next two and half-ish days of the seminar are about more mental work and also finances and health and other stuff. We pop in and out, leave early, and skip much of the final day and a half. Watching Robbins remains compelling—the man's an artist—but the subject matter is less interesting. I have walked. I have done what I came to do. No one else feels compelled to stay, either. So we leave.

We go to lunch and dinner together instead. We watch light on the river behind my brother's house and tell jokes and feel good together in the early spring sun.

Unveiling Hope

by Penne Lynne Richards

(Author's note: This account is based on extensive interviews conducted over three years with Jami and Jenna Slim and their mother, Angie Romans. Where possible, the facts have been independently verified.)

I have become so unhappy. I don't want this life anymore. – Jami

Sweat collects under the hijab that hides her long brown hair. The crowded bus emits a pungent odor of stale sweat and garlic, but she is not offended. Jami glances at her sister, Jenna, who does not wear a hijab; her sunlit mane flows to her waist. Freedom not to wear the hijab was a birthday gift from their Dad this year, when Jenna turned fifteen. She begged for it tirelessly. Funny, Jami never considered asking for such a lofty present.

Kacy, the sisters' dear friend and neighbor, has stolen away in support of their escape. She is traveling to Beirut to see them safely board the flight to America, then she will return to Komatieh, their village. Jami was seven, Jenna was five, and Jessica only two when their dad kidnapped them from St. Thomas, Canada, after he and their mother divorced. During his weekend visitation, instead of going to his apartment he took them to the airport to board a flight to Beirut, Lebanon. He told the girls that their mom would join them later. She didn't, but over the years she could call them.

"Hello, Mommy, can you bring my water gun when you come," Jami would beg.

"Honey, Mommy can't come right now. It's not safe right now," Mom would say.

"But Dad said you are coming on the plane to live with us. Why won't you come? I miss you, Mommy. Please, when are you coming?"

"Sweetheart, Mommy loves you so much. You don't ever forget that. No matter how long it takes me to see you. Don't forget, I love you! Promise me you won't forget," Mom would cry.

"I hate you! You are a liar! You aren't coming. You are just saying that. You just don't want to be with us," Jami would scream.

Jami didn't mean any of the things she said to Mom. She knew Mom didn't believe the hurtful words, either, because Mom kept calling, every week without fail.

Jami is old enough to remember Mom, before they were separated—her smile, the sound of her laughter, her warm hugs and her blue-green eyes, always sparkling. Living without her has been agony.

Sneaking away from school this morning without the guards noticing was a pure miracle. Finding the bus route and a driver was tricky, since Dad is also a bus driver. They all know him. The girls pay bus fare with the spare *Lira* they have collected and some American money they took from their Dad's closet. It's money Mom sent to them, but that he kept.

The first leg of their journey got them two blocks down the road, then the van overheated. Farther down the street they manage to board a larger bus to carry them the full thirty-five minute trip to Beirut.

Jessica, now 12, is not with them. Their situation is risky enough. Age 16 and 15, Jami and her younger sister Jenna are barely old enough to leave the country by themselves. Making it through airport security will be challenging. Even saying goodbye to Jessica would have been too dangerous.

Jami's knees scrape the back of the seat as she wiggles into a more comfortable position. The three are squished together on one seat. Cheeks pressing up against the window, Jami stares out trying not to think any more about Jessica. Up ahead, two cars have stopped in the middle of the road, and one driver jumps out yelling at the other driver. She sighs as their bus steers around the congestion. Street vendors line the sidewalks shoulder to shoulder selling vegetables, jewelry, fabrics. She wonders if she'll ever come back.

Jenna breaks into her thoughts. "Jami, what are you staring at?"

"Nothing. Everything," she tells her. "I don't want to forget, but I can hardly wait to leave."

"I have dreamt of this moment for so long. I always believed it would come true," Jenna says.

Kacy leans toward them, smiles, and cups her hands over theirs gently squeezing. "This is it! Jenna, Jami. You are really doing this. Finally after all the planning, you are escaping. This time it is real. Not like last time."

Jenna's green eyes flash. "This time the escape is our choice! Dad can't hurt us anymore. Not now. Not ever. But the best part of all, we are finally going to be with Mom!"

Their giddy chatter continues as if they have a million things to share and only one moment to say it all. As the bus approaches Beirut, time seems to slip away more and more quickly. They catch each other's giggles like a bad cold, and Jami locks eyes with an elderly lady sitting across the aisle from them. The lady reminds her of her grandmother. Her disapproving eyes are the color of her black scarf and it's difficult to tell where the scarf ends and her black smock top begins. Jami doesn't care. This is *their* adventure. No one can ruin it.

She leans her head against the window again and closes her eyes, hoping the sunshine will calm her thoughts, soothe her into sleep. When was the last time she polished the kitchen floor? Who would do this now? She doesn't care. That's no longer her job. Random feelings trickle through her mind as she drifts off.

Memories of the fight they had with Dad a month ago pummel her mind. His unpredictable mood swings and anger frightened her. On rare occasions she had seen him relaxed, enjoying his family.

But mostly—especially after the divorce—she remembers him being irritable, angry, yelling. She remembers him striking out toward her and Jenna—to Jenna more often because she can't keep her words inside her mouth. Jenna tried to act tough, like it didn't hurt. But her words were the match that ignited Dad's fury.

***

I remember him saying he loved me, but only once. – Jami

As the bus jostles them down the road, Jami attempts to stop her thoughts from rewinding to last month's fight with their dad.

"Get out," he roared as the sun set over their apartment building. "I don't care where you go—even if it's to your Mom. Get out! I don't want you here!"

His angry words pierced their ears, its meaning seeping in as they rushed to their room. Only one other time had he had thrown them out like this, but they were much younger and they didn't understand it.

They didn't wait to see where he went. They did not speak. Their hearts raced and their hands shook as they packed, paying little attention to the items they hurled into their bags. Jami tossed one shoe in and didn't bother to find the mate. It happened so fast she didn't notice what Jessica and her stepbrothers were doing. Mostly, when their Dad raged, they hid—in their bed, under the covers.

Fifteen minutes later, bags in hand, they made their exit without turning back. Jami didn't give a thought to the dirty dishes still in the sink. Barely down one flight of stairs, they realized that their bags were too heavy to carry much farther. They stashed them behind the stairwell closet on the ground floor, across from their grandparents' apartment.

"We can get it later. If we need it," Jami whispered. They knew if their grandparents saw them they would run to tell Dad.

"Let's go to the Kacy's building—to the roof," Jenna said. "She said there's an empty apartment there, and we can get a key from her later. It should be safe."

Their eagerness carried them to the apartments next door. Without attracting suspicion, they slipped through the door to the stairwell and climbed five flights to the roof, where they hid behind the shed that housed the water tank.

Jami's eyes panned the horizon like a camera documenting a story. Beyond the walls and the rooftops, the majestic mountains surrounding their village and the chiseled silhouettes of buildings comforted them like a familiar blanket. They sat on the cold concrete, propping themselves against the wall and facing the exit door, a possible escape route.

"We can't stay here forever," Jami said, her older-sister authority rising within her. "We need a plan. If we don't get some help, eventually Dad will find us. It should be safe to stay here through the night. We'll find Kacy in the morning. Maybe she can help."

Jenna popped up and began pacing, her tempo increasing with her agitation.

"I can't go back!" she announced. "One way or another, I have to find a way out—away from, Dad. I'm working on a real escape."

"I know how hard it is, and I'm ready to leave, too."

After burning off her nervous energy, Jenna sat and rested her head on Jami's shoulder.

"If this doesn't work out, I won't go back home. I just can't," she said.

Nightfall crept around them. They had no idea what to do next. Their plan was as empty as their stomachs.

"Do you smell that," Jenna asked finally, breaking the silence.

They inhaled the fragrance of meat and cinnamon. It was as though the whole building were having kafta. This made their hunger fiercer.

Frogs began croaking their evening lullaby. Jenna nodded off while Jami stared at the stars, no longer feeling the concrete beneath her. She didn't remember dozing off, either, but as she gazed at the moon, the night fled and made way for the day. It was a serene moment but it didn't last. Whatever peace the night brought was quickly replaced by the shock of waking in a strange place. It took them a moment to regain their wits. The crisp November air cooled them, and they were glad to have their jackets. The sun was still behind the clouds and the moon had disappeared into a rosy dawn. Instinctively, they placed their fingers over their lips, making a silent *shh*. Then they laughed. Jenna knuckled the sleep from her eyes and ran her fingers through her blonde hair, brushing it back into a secure ponytail.

"Maybe Kacy is up and getting ready for school," she said. "Let's go try to catch her before she leaves. She should have a key to her neighbors' vacation apartment and we can hide there," she said. The apartment belonged to a Swedish couple.

"How long will they be gone?"

"A few weeks, I think."

Dusting off their clothes, they left the roof and crept down the stairwell to the third floor, Kacy's floor. As if on cue, Kacy walked out of her apartment. They waved to her and ducked back into the stairwell.

"What are you doing here?" Kacy asked, hugging them both. She could barely keep from squealing. "Are you running away?"

"We slept on the roof of your building," Jenna said. "But now we need a new place to stay until we figure out what to do next. Can you get us into your neighbors' apartment on the fourth floor?"

"Their place would be perfect," Jami said. "But we have to hurry and get out of here."

"Go ahead and go upstairs," Kacy said. "I'll get a key and meet you up there in a few minutes. There's no way I'm going to the university today with all this excitement going on."

Kacy's neighbors' apartment was decorated with upscale art work. Exquisite rugs warmed the polished marble floors. Every inch was pristine. The sun peeked in a window and Jami glimpsed her reflection in the marble as she crossed through the kitchen to the bedroom.

For a moment she thought of their kitchen, Dad's kitchen. It was normal for her to spend hours after school cleaning and scrubbing the floor-to-ceiling marble until it gleamed. From an early age, deep cleaning their home was expected of her. It was more than an obligation; she *wanted* to keep it clean. To make Dad proud of their home—and of her.

"Daddy, you are home so late," Jami would say. "I kept some mjadra warm for you. Here, sit down at the table and relax while you eat," she would say anxiously.

"Is this all you cooked?" he would shout. "It's not even a full meal. Where's my salata? Did you make fries? We have a kitchen full of food, but you can't cook enough for me?"

"I will make you a salata right now, Daddy. Did you notice I buffed the kitchen floors?"

"Did you clean under the stove?"

When she was 12 one day he told her he loved her. It was in passing, and she was so shocked that she almost missed it. And that was all—gone in a blink. She never heard it again.

They went into the Swedes' bedroom and climbed into the king-sized bed, all three of them. The night had been so short for Jenna and Jami, but they were still running on adrenaline. Quickly they brought Kacy up to speed and, as they chatted, their giggles faded into a blissful, deep sleep.

Rap, rap, rap! Knuckles rattled against the apartment door, but still they slept. "Kacy, are you and the Slim girls in there?" Kacy's Mom called from the hallway. "Kacy, open up. Let me help."

They tossed in their slumbers and dreamily heard a distant voice. The hours slowly drifted by.

The growling of Jami's stomach finally awakened her. Jenna and Kacy began to stir.

Suddenly—*bang, bang, bang* on the door. Frozen, they stared at each other. *Bang, bang, bang...*

"We know you are in there," Jessica and their stepbrothers shouted in unison.

"Open the door! I know you are in there," Dad yelled. "I'll get the police to come break down this door."

They huddled in the bed.

"Shh," Jenna whispered. "Maybe they'll give up if we are quiet."

The banging went on for what seemed like forever. Then as quickly as it began, it stopped. They stared at each other until Jami broke the spell.

"I don't know what will happen next, but soon we have to go home and pray for the best."

"Please, let's just stay here a while longer," Jenna pleaded. "We are already in trouble, so why should we rush? If we really think hard, we can find a way out. Please, Jami."

"Maybe I can talk to my Mom?" Kacy suggested. "I can ask her to meet us at your apartment. With her there it might keep your Dad from blowing up like he always does. It's worth a try."

Resolved to face the situation together, they left the apartment behind.

The sun had set when they entered the first floor of their building and retrieved the luggage they had left behind the stairs. White-knuckled from gripping their bags, they began their ascent. Halfway up the second floor, they recognized their Dad sitting on one of the steps, just in front of their doorway. A deep moan engulfed their ears. They were caught, not in a fury of rants, but in a cry of relief. They had been prepared to cower under his 6-foot-frame, like lambs at a slaughter. Instead, he simply ushered them into the apartment. Jessica stood in the hallway near their bedroom and her stepbrothers near the living room, all of them caught off guard.

"You came home," Dad wailed. "I didn't think you would ever come home. I thought you were gone forever."

There wasn't time for a reply. The phone saved them. Dad cleared his throat as he answered the call, and they took the opening to put their bags in their bedroom. They smiled at Jessica, and she nodded.

They caught only his side of the conversation, then he stopped talking and, covering the phone with his right hand, shoved it to Jami.

"I was so worried that I called the American Embassy looking for you," he told her. "Now you have to fix it! Tell her that everything is fine and you are OK. Say that you were only skipping school for fun." He droped the phone into her hand.

She answered in Arabic. "Hello? Yes, my name is Jami Slim." A female voice was on the other end. "I am all right, thank you. We only skipped school for fun, and we are so sorry to worry our Dad." She wondered why this nice lady seemed so concerned about her and Jenna.

"I don't mean to interrupt, but where did you say you are calling from," Jami asked. "I've never heard of the American Embassy. Are you in America? Beirut, really? I don't know about your American Embassy. Yes, I'm sure we are OK, *shukran*. Of course you can talk to my sister."

Jami passed the phone to Jenna.

"Hi, yes, my name is Jenna Slim," Jenna answered, the usual smile in her voice. She turned her back from her Dad's watchful eyes. "Can you repeat that again? I didn't hear you very well." She listened intently to memorize, as Jami later learned, the Embassy's phone number the woman provided.

"Yes, we are fine. We didn't mean to make any trouble," Jenna said. "It was nice to talk to you, too. *Shukran* for calling." Jenna turned to face her Dad.

"Now," he said, "put your things away and clean up the kitchen if you want any dinner. You're hungry, aren't you? What have you eaten today?"

Without another word he turned for his room. There was a sickening feeling in their stomachs, and they knew this wasn't the end.

But the time would come. A door had opened at last, a door their Dad had naively opened. The woman that called to check on them—her voice was so pleasant, reassuring. Maybe she could help them get to their Mom. What was this American Embassy? Why had their Dad called them when he thought they weren't coming back? Now, it seemed, they had someone on their side.

From that night forward and each time Jenna fought with their dad, which was often, she would call the Embassy lady. She told how they had been kidnapped. On those occasions when she couldn't call herself, Kacy called for her.

***

I'm a dreamer. I have visualized from a very young age how to leave. – Jenna

As the driver steers the bus toward Beirut, Jenna's mind oscillates between their excitement, now that they are on their way, and a month ago when Dad kicked them out of the house, and finally to last night when everything fell into place.

Finally, Jenna had proof. She had remained calm enough to record their dad during their fight. It's one thing for a girl to explain how bad her life is, but it's completely different when she has evidence. It's taken almost ten years, but she always believed they'd get out of here.

This past year, especially these last months, Jenna and Jami have been learning to cope with their situation by praying, the way their Mom taught them. During their Sunday phone calls, Mom talked about having something called faith.

Jenna could almost hear her mom's voice: *I know God is moving and going to bring you back to me. You start saying the same thing out loud to each other, and you believe it in your heart. Don't doubt it, ever!* Mom reminded her.

Faith is a part of their mother and it is becoming a part of them. Their Dad has never spoken of God. When Jenna was younger, a few years after Dad took them from St. Thomas and brought them to Lebanon, she would walk to the Mosque and watch people. Most went inside to pray, but she'd stayed outside. Sometimes she would kneel on the ground and bow her head on a rock, trying to mimic the ritual of prayer. At night she enjoyed sitting on the apartment balcony looking at the moon. Jenna believed the moon was God's house, and He would sit down and dangle His feet over the edge to watch over them. She dreamed of finding a piece of wood large enough to float her across the ocean, back to her Mom.

The bus lurches to the left, jostling her attention back to Jami and Kacy.

"Jami," she nudges her sister with her shoulder. "Are you thinking about last night, too?"

"Yeah, hard not to. Are you OK?" Jami asks.

"I'm better than OK. I'm great. I knew our plan would work. With this evidence, everyone will believe us. I really didn't even feel his hand slapping my face. It was like being in a dream. You know, when everything is in slow motion and without feeling." Jenna's grin widens. "Why do you ask?"

"Oh, you just seem far off." Jami looks at her and starts to reach for Jenna's cheek. "So you aren't hurt?"

Jenna impulsively brushes her hand away. "I can't stop thinking about last night. I believe with all my heart that it's not an accident that our plan worked so smoothly! An even bigger miracle happened when Dad called me back to his room this morning to say he was sorry. He never apologizes. I'd been praying for a way to say goodbye, without him knowing I was leaving. When he did that, I knew that was my goodbye."

"But weren't you so scared Dad would catch you stealing the passports?" Jami asks. "I held my breath the whole time and prayed he wouldn't hear you."

The bus slows to a halt at the next stop and more passengers push onto the already crowded ride. More than half are standing. Arabic chatter rises another decibel. One final stop before they reach the church in Beirut, their appointed destination.

Yesterday, after Jenna realized Dad knew she had skipped school, she decided to risk everything. She desperately wanted the proof that would get her out of Lebanon. If she didn't try, the chance to try again might not come for a long time. Be brave, she told herself.

She had dressed as if she planned to go to school; instead, she went to Kacy's apartment to hang out, listen to music and hide. Jami took Jessica and their twin step-brothers to school, as usual. By late morning Jenna decided it was safe to go back to her own apartment until her brothers and sisters walked home from school. The unusually cold December temperatures made way for the occasional rain showers. As she relaxed in her pajamas, she heard footsteps clomping up the stairs toward the front door.

"Jenna," Jami said breathlessly, "Dad picked us up from school and he's parking the car."

"You're in trouble," Jessica said as she hurried out of the kitchen to the bedroom.

"Yah, Dad is so mad," the twins taunted.

"Good! I don't care," Jenna said as she raced to her room, Jami two steps behind her.

"What are you going to do?"

"I'm getting the recorder. I put fresh batteries in it, and it's fully charged." Jenna steadied her hands as she tucked the hand-held device inside the top of her pajamas to hide it. She knew she didn't have much time.

"Jenna, I don't know if this is a good idea."

"I do. This will be all the proof I need. You don't want to be in here when he comes in. I'll be OK, promise."

"Please be careful."

Determination filled her. This will work, Jenna told herself. This will be her ticket out.

Her index finger hit the record button. She busied herself filling the water bottles in the corner of the kitchen. She was ready. Dad exploded into the apartment.

The first slap came down solid on her left cheek.

Next, a backhanded slap across her right cheek.

By the time the third strike landed, she had willed herself not to feel it.

Each strike stung less than the one before. She was numb when it ended, leaving her in the center of the kitchen. Slowly, she made her way back to her bedroom.

"Jami, I got it all on tape," she whispered. "I'm leaving tomorrow. I'm going to get Kacy's attention from our balcony, and she can call the Embassy. I want to give them this tape. It should be enough to get me on a plane out of here."

"I'm going with you," Jami said, clutching her arm. "You aren't leaving me here to take the blame when you're gone."

"I want you to come, but if you change your mind, I'm still leaving."

"I know you will, but I'm sure—I'm coming, too."

Jenna glanced out the bedroom door to listen for any movement before slipping into the hallway. The silence satisfied her. Returning to her room, she walked to the glass door leading to the balcony. She traced her hand over the cool metal handle to steady her willpower. She listened again and turned the handle. December's mountain air and the singing crickets and frogs recharged her. *This is what I will miss—Lebanon*, she realized.

"Psst, psst, Kacy," she whispered in the direction of Kacy's balcony. She glanced back into her apartment. "Kacy," she hissed again, leaning over the edge to throw her voice toward Kacy's ears. "Kaaacccy," she mustered once more. Finally, she spotted a profile. *Please, God, let it be, Kacy,* she exhaled.

"Jenna, what are you doing?" Kacy whispered.

"*Yalla,* I need your help. Can you call the Embassy, now? Tell them that I have a recording of my dad— Dad hitting me. I am running away tomorrow morning, and Jami said she is coming, too. Ask them what we will need to get on an airplane to America. I'll wait here. *Yalla.*"

"OK, I'll be back."

Crouching on the balcony, the full moon seemed to expose her like an X-ray machine: Her scars. Her pain. "God, I don't know if you are up there, but if you can hear me, I want to go home to be with my mom. If I do go, show me the way to say a silent goodbye to my dad. Give me a sign to know when it's my goodbye. Fill me with peace so I know it's settled inside of me." *Shukran*, she mouthed to the heavens. She dabbed the corners of her eyes with the sleeve of her shirt. The mountaintops seemed to grow larger as the moon's shadow played off their peaks.

"Jenna, are you still there?" Kacy whispered.

Jenna leaned forward. "What did they say?"

"You need your passports—and your birth certificates, if you can get them. They will meet you after the third bus stop in Beirut—the one across from the church. You know the place? But I want to ride with you tomorrow. Can I?"

"Fine with me. I will see you in the morning. *Shukran*, Kacy." She waved goodnight.

Jenna asked Jami to stand guard while she made her way into Dad's empty room. He was dozing on he couch. They agreed that if he started coming into the room, Jami would call out the twins' names to warn her.

The room was dark and she had to navigate with her arms and hands stretched out in front of her until she reached the opening of his closet. She managed to glide her hands over the boxes on the top shelf. She had no idea which box contained the passports, and in her eagerness the weight of her hand dislodged one of the boxes, causing it to tumble into her outstretched arms. She crouched on the floor, waiting for the noise to reach her Dad.

"*Yalla*! Did you find them," Jami hissed from the hallway.

She couldn't speak. By now, her eyes had adjusted to the darkness. Peering into the box, she saw all of their passports stacked inside. She found hers and then Jami's. For a moment she considered taking Dad's, too, so he couldn't follow them, then decided against it.

Quickly she grabbed the two passports, replaced the box on the shelf, and hurried out of the room.

"I got them," Jenna said under her breath, sweeping past Jami on the way to the bedroom.

"I can hardly believe this is happening," Jami whispered, following her.

Jenna kept smiling. "I'm full of freaky bubbles, but it feels good. Here, put this in your backpack," she said as she handed over Jami's passport.

"*Shukran*. Let's be smart and plan this right. Only pack a few things that are special—things we don't want to leave behind. It will look like we are packed for school." Jami said.

"Sneaky, I like it." The thought made her smile even more. But as she rested her head on her pillow, her smile weakened. She touched her cheek, quickly before Jami saw her. Why does he hit, she wondered.

She watched Jami slide a box not much larger than a shoebox from beneath the bed and removed the lid to reveal her treasures: a few necklaces, bracelets, some *Lira*, music cassette tapes, journals, a book of poems, a calendar, two bottles of cologne, stationary for writing. Gently, Jami transferred them into her backpack.

"Jenna, come here," Dad called from his bedroom.

The girls stared at each other, Jenna's heart racing.

"What if he sees the passports missing? What are we going to do," Jami said.

"It doesn't matter. Nothing is changing. I'll be back. Don't be scared."

She walked slowly to his room. Be brave, she told herself. "Yes, sir, did you call me?"

"I am sorry for what happened last night," he said as he hugged her. "I didn't mean to hurt you."

"*Shukran*. It's OK," she said as she tapped his back. She knew it would never happen again. And she knew this was her goodbye. A calm filled her.

***

I used to watch the airplanes from my balcony, and knew that one day I'd be on one. – Jenna

The bus slows to a halt next to the church where they are to meet Herro, the lady from the Embassy. The driver opens the doors and they gather their backpacks and make their way out. The three girls stand at the curb and watch the bus slowly pull away. Jenna turns back toward their meeting place, the church, and notices a midnight-blue SUV that wasn't there before. Quickly, she glances at Jami, then at Kacy to see if they have noticed. Jami turns to face the church as a gentle December breeze lifts her hijab, ever so slightly, from her shoulders.

Softly she reaches for the ties, and her hands effortlessly free it from her head.

Build it and They Will Come

by Pamela Skjolsvik

(*Note: The names in this piece have been changed to protect the innocent and the guilty.*)

"Let's wake the bastards up," are the first words I hear. I've entered the darkened control room that looks out onto the inmate population of the county jail, and within thirty seconds I realize that I'm going to have a huge problem fitting in.

I take a seat in one of the empty chairs, my presence ignored by the four uniformed deputies, including Corporal McCully. He is one of five people who interviewed me for the position. After about ten minutes, he informs me that Carla, the woman training me, is late. Another five minutes pass, and Carla breezes into the room. Hair bleached blonde, colorful clothes, and lime-green Croc sandals, she is the physical antithesis of the other deputies. With her presence, I feel less alone and, for some reason, less guilty, relieved at where I've found myself—behind bars.

Training

"It's best not to know what they're in for," Carla advises as we walk toward the kitchen for breakfast, one of three free meals offered during my shift. Impossible. Not only do I want to know who I'm handing over the Honey Buns to when I'm delivering commissary orders, I'm more curious than a 5-year-old kid on Christmas Eve. My job title, detention specialist, is kind of misleading, because I don't know exactly what I'm specializing in. My daily duties include not only ordering commissary items and phone cards, but also creating the court list of new arrests, accounting for the inmates' funds and running to the library to pick up their weekly book requests. And there's an occasional warrant that I need to modify in the computer system. But mostly I'm a glorified gofer for the guys and gals behind bars.

When Carla gives me my first tour of the facility, every eye watches me like I'm parading around in the nude, and I feel my body tense and my temperature go up a notch. Being the new person is kind of cool at a regular place of employment, like an insurance agency. But when you're dealing with men who have been locked up for months, it's creepy.

Our first stop is the five-hundred block, the special management cases. Carla warns me that I should bring along a deputy whenever I step inside this unit because it houses the men incarcerated for the most serious offenses. As we step into the concrete holding pen, she introduces me as though I'm the next contestant in the Miss America pageant. The ten men peer from behind bars to get a better look at me. I meekly say hello, do a little half-wave and turn to leave.

"Who's in there?" I ask as the gate clangs behind us.

"You really want to know?" She says this like a woman in a sewing circle, eager to share the juiciest piece of gossip.

"Well, yeah."

"The guy on the end is Ben Wahler. He used to be a sheriff and a foster parent. I think he had over one hundred kids over the years. Anyway, he's in here for sexual assault on a child."

My mouth drops open.

"Oh, and one more thing. You can't tell anyone, like your husband or friends, about the people in here. The only thing you can tell about an inmate is their offense and bond amount. That's it. Especially if you want to be a deputy, cause during your polygraph, they'll ask you if you've revealed any confidential information."

When I get home that night, I Google the name of the molester. I am shocked and disgusted by what I find. But I've got to put my natural instincts away if I want to perform the duties of my job. I find out on Wednesday, commissary day, that he is one of the lucky inmates who has money on his books. Among the items in his order are fire hot Jolly Ranchers, a drawing tablet and Gardetto's corn chips. When we approach his cell, I half expect to find the devil himself with sharp pointy horns sprouting from his head. Instead I find a tall, balding man reminiscent of the Pillsbury Doughboy, with a soft lilting voice. He informs Carla that he's going to draw a picture for his daughter.

As we continue the deliveries, I find that the inmates are very respectful. They call me Ma'am and say thank you, like I've just pardoned them. Their formal sincerity makes me feel older than my years, but I'm not going to insist they call me Miss or by my name. We are playing the game of institutionalization: Be nice to the woman who holds your bag of Cheetos, and she'll be nice to you.

After each delivery, the inmate must sign his name on the sales slip with a pencil stating that he has received all of his items. We all touch this little golf pencil, and as soon as we're finished with deliveries, I wash my hands with an OCD-like fervor. Later that day, the nurse calls me into her office to give me a TB test and a vaccination for hepatitis B. The following week, I don a pair of surgical gloves, which amuses most of the inmates, like I'm some candy-carrying nurse there to give them a rectal exam. I tell them it's flu season. What they fail to realize—or maybe they do—is that only I am protected from the germ-ridden pencil. They have virtually touched every inmate's penis in the joint.

Hygiene, especially of the dental variety, isn't a huge priority among the inmates. I can only surmise from this that their bad breath is a defense mechanism to ward off the unwanted advances by love-hungry fellow inmates. Either that, or they have never adopted a tooth-brushing routine into their daily regimen, and they entered the facility with a mouthful of gingivitis and cavities. To freshen the air between us, I chew minty gum and breathe through my mouth. BO isn't really a problem, at least from where I stand, because they do buy soap. They have two choices: good old-fashioned Ivory or the nauseatingly scented Irish Spring, which seems to be the soap of choice among male inmates. I guess no one wants to be perceived as an Ivory girl around here, even among the women.

"Tough" or "been around the block a few times" are just two ways to describe the few women at the county jail. The majority are in for drug-related offenses, mostly meth, which, as side effects, rots their teeth, making them look way older than they are, and dots their skin with angry acne. If there is any compensation for their affliction, they are slender and, for now, sober.

On my third day of training I see a familiar female face pass by the control room window, making her way towards the female housing unit. She is my kids' pediatrician, a woman I like and totally respect. I panic and duck out of view.

"Oh, my God, is that Kelly Harrington?"

One of the male deputies looks at me disapprovingly over his newspaper. "Yep. She's been in here a couple of times."

"For what?!?"

"She's got issues with her ex-husband."

"Oh," I sigh, thankful that it isn't for doing something harmful to kids. She will be here only one night, and I inform everyone I work with that I don't want her to see me. It would be too uncomfortable and weird the next time I take my kids in for a checkup or a flu shot.

Carla trains me for four weeks, and at the end I still don't feel confident enough to handle the job on my own. Dealing with the inmates isn't the problem. It's the temperamental computer system that I use to check criminal histories and warrant information that intimidates the hell out of me. The system is not user-friendly; barely any of the deputies know how to operate it, which I find rather strange.

"You're the Detention Specialist," one of the older male deputies quips after I've tried to modify a warrant several times and finally asked for assistance. His attitude echoes that of most of the deputies, but since he's dating the female lieutenant, who outranks them all, he feels empowered say whatever pops into his mind. Everyone is afraid to point out his less than stellar work ethic because they fear retribution. Unbeknownst to his girlfriend the lieutenant, he is frequently on the control room computer watching a raunchy video of the Pussycat Dolls shaking their scantily clad bodies.

Sexual innuendo, foul language and inappropriate conduct are a daily occurrence at the jail. And it's the employees, not the inmates, who are guilty. I am not a puritan, and I've worked plenty of jobs where inappropriate behavior was not only accepted but encouraged. My problem is that I feel the conduct of jail employees should be above reproach if we are to set any kind of example. It is beyond annoying to sit in a room full of supposed professionals, sober people, who can't verbalize without interjecting "fuck" into every sentence.

One day, as I order the inmates' books from the library, I come across a request for *Leaves of Grass* by Walt Whitman. I share my excitement with a male deputy, as I'm tired of seeing all the requests for Patterson, Koontz and King—the standard jail reading fare.

"What? Is it a book about pot?"

"Actually, it's a book of poetry. You know, using the English language to paint a picture, instead of using it to sound ugly and uneducated?"

"So, who's the fucking fag who wants that?"

The female deputies aren't much better. To fit in with the boys' club at the county jail, they've adopted an over-the-top hardness, especially in their dealings with female inmates. They strut and attempt a badass demeanor, but to me they're about as menacing as John Travolta in *Saturday Night Fever*. During my first week of work, one of them shows a video of a naked female magician. It is cute and clever, but not appropriate for any kind of work environment, and I am sickened as everyone stands around commenting on the woman's tits and ass.

For now, Carla remains free of affectation. "I'm not here to judge these people," she says to me one day after dealing with an inmate who refused to be transported to prison with Ben Wahler, the child molester. "They've already been judged in a court of law."

But judgment appears to be a job duty of the deputy. As I place a weekly commissary order, I come across an inmate who indicates on his form that he wishes to purchase a pair of women's underwear. Out of curiosity, I pull the man's booking card to see what he's in for, what he looks like and where he's housed. The inmate, Mr. William Begay, is a Native American with long black hair, carefully applied cat-girl eyeliner and a formidable set of hormone-produced man boobs. He's in for domestic violence against his boyfriend, who is housed a mere twenty feet away in another unit at the jail. Mr. Begay is all alone in a special solitary cell because he is a pre-op transsexual, not to mention seriously delusional for thinking he could squeeze his 5-foot-10, 220-pound body into a woman's size 7 Hanes Her Way pair of panties.

Being the people pleaser that I am, I ask one of the deputies if I should order Mr. Begay the XL "big girl" undies, or should I just order what he put on the sheet. The room becomes silent and as Deputy Whittaker's jaw drops, I swear I can hear the theme song from *The Good, the Bad and the Ugly* begin to play.

"What...did...you...just...say?" He draws out each word for dramatic effect.

"Should I just go ahead and order the extra large? Because there is no way in hell that he'll fit in a medium."

"Men can't order women's underwear."

"Well, isn't he on his way to becoming a woman?"

"He's still got a dick."

"Yeah, but he's got bigger boobs than I do."

Deputies giggle.

"The *It* gets men's briefs. End of story." Whittaker's face is flushed. I shouldn't continue with the argument, but I can't help myself.

"How come all the women get to order boxers?"

"Because..."

Whittaker is at a loss for words. Corporal McCully saves him, interjecting "because they wear them as pajamas."

"Well, maybe Mr. Begay wants to sleep in some women's underwear. What's the big deal?"

Carla decides to settle this argument. She checks with Sergeant Howard, who handles administrative policy at the jail, and he agrees that women shouldn't be able to order boxers. Two days later, the shit hits the fan when Whittaker bellyaches to the lieutenant that he doesn't want to see all these skanky women in their tiny underwear at bed check, and that them having boxers is the only way to protect his aesthetic sensibilities. It's a crock, but it flies and for once the double standard works in favor of women.

Even though my coworkers and I are not technically "in jail," the undeniable affects of institutionalization still manifest themselves. "I'm not Racist, I Hate Everyone," should be elegantly embroidered on the front of all deputies' uniforms, right beneath their names. Since there is not a lot of ethnic, cultural or religious diversity where I live, everyone I work with assumes that I am Republican, Christian and intolerant of gay marriage and gay people in general, with the exception of the lesbians that work for the sheriff's office. During my first week of work, I unwisely decide to eat my lunch in the break room with my peers. As I plop my plate down on the table, the female undersheriff looks me up and down as if she knows me but can't remember how.

"Where do you go to church?" she asks. " You look so familiar."

"I don't," I reply, wrangling a scoop of jello into my mouth. From the reaction of the other people at the table, this is not the correct response. I might as well have said I was orchestrating a human sacrifice and was wondering where I might find a couple of goats and a virgin.

"Where do you go to church?" I ask out of politeness, but more to break the awkward silence.

When she tells me the name of her church, I say that I've been there a couple of times for craft shows. This may not be connection she is hoping for, so I wolf down my lunch and make a speedy exit. I imagine that the minute I leave the room, people will begin to plot my demise, as it is becoming glaringly apparent to the people I work with that I am not one of them.

The Beginning of the End

I become an official outsider on my favorite holiday, Halloween, a day on which there is no obligation to exchange presents, attend church services or travel hundreds of miles out of familial obligation and guilt. All you have to do is put on a costume, get a bag, go out among your neighbors and let your kids rake in the free candy.

And so when I have to work on my favorite holiday, and I can't even wear a costume, I am seriously bummed out. One of the more flirtatious and outspoken inmates asks me what costume I am going to wear. I inform him that employees of the sheriff's office aren't allowed to dress up, but that I'd be showing up as my evil twin.

"I hope your twin likes to wear mini skirts."

I don't wear a mini skirt, just an orange shirt with a pumpkin on it. All the deputies are kind of jumpy whenever I walk up behind them since the prison jumpsuit is orange. As quitting time approaches, I ask Deputy Connor, a hulking man with the temperament of Charlie Brown, if he is taking his daughter trick or treating.

"I'm going to go home, eat and go to bed. I hate Halloween."

To kill time as the deputies sit and wait for the next shift to arrive, I ramble on about my love of Halloween. When I finish, Connor adds, "I hate Christmas, too."

"Are you Jewish?" I ask.

Deputy Johnson, one of the female deputies whose whole family seems to work for the sheriff's office in one capacity or another, lets out a shriek.

"I can't believe you just accused Connor of being a Jew."

My face flares into an expression that could melt a glacier. Accuse?

"*I'm* Jewish," I say. The room is silent, as no one knows exactly what to say. "Actually, I'm a Jew for Jesus."

I stand up, grab my purse and exit the room fuming. I'm not really Jewish, but I am shocked by her blatant anti-Semitism. Deputy Preston, a young, good-natured guy, tries to soften the blow of what just happened by insisting that I do a dance before he'll let me leave for the night. I'm so angry that I want to scream, but instead, I do a little jig as the door buzzes, and I rush out into the cool night air.

As if it couldn't get any worse, my supervisor, Sergeant Garcia, whom I've never met, starts to work the day shift. He is a compact man with a large head that sits on his shoulders without the assistance of a neck. He fancies himself a country musician and tortures the night shift with his guitar playing. Fortunately, during the day, the serenades aren't allowed. He hates working days and reminds everyone around him of this on a nonstop basis. Within the week, he calls Andrea, the other detention specialist, and me into a meeting.

"The lieutenant and I feel that you both weren't trained properly, and with the upcoming jail expansion we need to fix that. We need both of you to work the night shift for a month or longer and be trained again by Deputy Johnson."

Oh joy. The anti-Semite.

"I can't do that. I've got kids, and daycare is next to impossible to find," I plead.

"You can take it up with the lieutenant, but I need both of you to go through the training again."

I immediately talk to the female lieutenant, explaining that working nights is not feasible for me. I further explain that my husband is turning forty, and it's the holidays and my family is all coming in for Christmas. She says she'll talk to the captain. Within a week, we are called in again. The lieutenant and Sergeant Garcia look at Andrea and me as if we are very naughty children.

"The undersheriff said you'll have to do the training," Lieutenant Marsten states in a matter-of-fact tone.

"What am I going to do with my kids? I mean, when I was offered this job, no one ever said I'd have to work a night shift. If they had, I wouldn't have taken the job."

"This is law enforcement. If there was an emergency here at 2 in the morning, who do you think we'd call?" she says.

"Who?" I ask innocently.

They look at each other and smile. "You."

This is news to me.

"But I have kids."

"That's not our problem, and I really can't relate. I really can't," the lieutenant says.

Of course you can't, I want to say, but I don't have the guts. This woman stands about 4 feet tall, yet her heartless uncaring demeanor makes *me* feel small and helpless.

"Maybe law enforcement isn't for you," she continues. My eyes well up with tears, not because I will miss out on the glorious opportunity of one day rising through the ranks of the sheriff's office, but because I feel as disposable and disliked as one of the inmates.

Exit

Allen Johnson's pock-marked, expressionless face stares out at me from the window of his new cell, situated directly in front of the control room door, a door that I must exit at least twenty times a day. He's dressed in a dark green, tear-proof gown that looks like a heavy winter coat that a matronly woman in North Dakota might wear over her church clothes. For the past 48 hours, he's been on suicide watch, after he informed the nurse that he had a long necklace in his possession that he planned on hanging himself with. Even though a heavy steel door separates us, his dark vacant eyes bring out a primal fear response as they stare into mine, making me want to sprint away like a scared animal. He is awaiting trial for raping his 2-year-old niece with an axe handle.

"He's just a pussy," one of the deputies loudly proclaims entering the control room, fully aware that Mr. Johnson can hear him.

"If you really want to kill yourself, you don't tell anyone, you just do it," adds another. I don't say a word.

I realize now why I can't stay here. I can't change the fucked up system, and I refuse to become immune to it in order to survive the day. Because the jail serves several purposes—holding tank for trials, sentencing for misdemeanors and initial intake of all offenses—it is just a motley mix of messed up people. Most are harmless folks doing dumb things that really only hurt themselves and the ones they love. But sometimes you encounter true evil. I don't want to suppress my fear with false bravado; I want to toss a razor to Allen Johnson when no one is looking.

The following day, I draft my letter of resignation and leave it on Sergeant Garcia's desk. I'm not surprised that none of my coworkers begs me to stay or acknowledges the fact that I was squeezed out of a coveted county job during the holidays. They're used to people leaving, and they're always hiring in corrections. At the end of my shift on my final day, I leave without ceremony. As I'm buzzed out of the thick metal door, I am greeted by a couple of grumpy night shift deputies who are late for work. I smile widely at them as if I know something that they don't.

The Authors

Joanna Cattanach

Joanna Cattanach is a writer and journalism instructor in Dallas. She previously worked for *The Dallas Morning News* before leaving to become a freelance writer, blogger and instructor. Her work has appeared in *The Dallas Morning News*, local magazines and online. She has written a wide range of stories including regular op-ed pieces and feature stories most often written from first-hand experience. For example, a botched attempt at rattlesnake hunting and a brief, painful period as a roller derby girl. Cattanach is from Blum, Texas, and attended Baylor University where she graduated with her master's in journalism in 2006. She is married with one son and two feisty cats.

[story behind the story]

I met my biological father two weeks before my wedding and 25 years after he and my biological mother gave my brother and me up for adoption. To say that it was an awkward meeting would be an understatement. Maybe it was the writer in me, or the daughter in me, or the toddler in me who still wondered why he left, but I chose at that moment to reconnect, to rebuild, to reunite.

The past five years, our relationship has been strained. At times awkward, at times beautiful, at times my father will disappear for months and reappear wanting to know when he can see me again. He gives me little-girl birthday cards and stuffs a $5 bill inside though I'm 32 years old now with my own child. I screen my phone calls to avoid him but also find myself waiting for his familiar voice on Sunday evenings. He has angered me and worried me and once, when he disappeared, I spent a night searching through autopsy reports online hoping that he wasn't one of the unidentified Hispanic males in the morgue.

This is what reunion is like for us. And though some people have advised me to let go and move on, and admittedly I've tried, there is something about a good story, an unbelievable story, about discovering your past and being a part of that discovery that is far too tempting to resist.

How can I not write about this? So I have. I hope this story inspires you in the way that is has inspired me to hope that whatever is lost can be found. And to write about it.

Susan Fisher

Susan Fisher – moving lady (United Van Lines), Editor in Chief (*Billerica News*), waitress, lawyer, Media Coordinator for Madalyn Murray O'Hair, staff member at nation's first decriminalized alcoholism reception center – bumps into Mayborn, wins prize".

[story behind the story]

If ever there were a poster child for evidence of the capacity of a profession for independent judgment, I'm a great candidate for writers everywhere.

Dragged kicking and screaming into actual, heartfelt dedication to "craft" at Mayborn's School of Journalism, I learned at the age of 62 to be respectful of her third grade journals, of her first novel in fifth grade, and of the capacity for spiritual guidance not only in St. Augustine's confessions but in the screenplay of the movie *Bernie*.

My first course at Mayborn began with the adult version of "tell the class what you did this summer" when Conference leader George Getschow asked class members why they were in his narrative class. I answered "I'm a 60-year-old woman who needed a loan." The "poetry" of my response was honest and a pretty clear indication of the basement to which I had relegated my self-esteem as a writer.

I realize now that the paucity of my perspective was part and parcel of a cynicism to which I no longer ascribe: writing is a responsibility, a source of joy, an ethical standard, both personally and publicly, and disarmingly elementary: Pencil, paper, write.

My winning piece expressed an anguish about teen pregnancy which, if left unexpressed, is a great example of a useless, counterproductive acid on imagination and emotion. When molded into narrative, it becomes its own salve by virtue of the innate healing quality of sharing, plain and simple.

It was touching to be recognized publicly, but nothing beats the wonder of hearing another author (the esteemed writer Bill Marvel) say to me, "I've never really thought about what it feels like to be teething."

Join the community of hard work, late night self-doubt, that nagging "I haven't even *started* my science project, due this very weekend." Get in the line that says WRITERS and find some relief even as you dispense it. This line may often be impoverished but only materially: if you're curious, amenable to enthusiasm, learning, laughter and camaraderie, this is the line for you.

One of the best places to join that line is the Mayborn Conference.

Bring pencil, paper, and get ready to feel at home.

Amanda Griffith

Amanda Griffith has taught secondary English for 28 years in both middle and high school. She has written two young adult books and a nonfiction narrative. A chapter from *Child of South Vietnam* was published in the 2010 spring issue of *Kartika Review* and two other chapters will be published in *Ten Spurs* Volume 7. This segment won 3rd place in the Reported Narrative category in 2012 at the Mayborn Conference.

[story behind the story]

In the 1990s, modeling writing for my students in McKinney, Texas, inspired me to write a novel. The amazing thing about writing with my students is when they recognize my writing to be real and for a purpose, they become more excited in their own efforts.

Later in my writing career, with two young adult books completed, I told my stylist my plan to write nonfiction. She said, "You should write my story." I listened with half an ear until she shared some powerful moments from her childhood in Vietnam, such as a grandmother picking blueberries on the mountain and being blown to bits by an American sharpshooter from a military helicopter, and she and some friends encountering a Burmese python in her backyard actively chewing the remains of one of the family's chickens. What I didn't realize until later was that her story was of a mischievous young girl whose parents had lovingly guided into mature womanhood. This they did in as normal a way as possible while a war was fought on their doorstep.

During the last three years, I've interviewed Thái Le Nguyen and compiled research information to write her story of growing up in South Vietnam during the war. In the process, I have discovered my knack for reporting and for writing in the persona of my subject to be so flawless that when I arrived at my Mayborn workshops for the last two years, the participants who didn't know me were amazed the author of the book was an American co-writer.

For my students the last ten years, I have been a mentor for writing improvement and persistence as they hear of my quest to achieve publication. Someday, I tell them, they will hear of my book being published, but for now, I focus on the aspiration of more magazine publications, and I continue querying and revising, revising, revising.

Evan Moore

Evan Moore is a former newspaper and magazine writer and editor who has worked for the *Fort Worth Star-Telegram, The Dallas Morning News* and the *Houston Chronicle*. For five years, he and his wife, Dianna, were the owners and publishers of the weekly *Bosque County News*. Moore sold that paper in 2009. He's now the editor of the *Daily World* in Opelousas, Louisiana. A number of Moore's essays have been published in Sunday magazines and a collection of them is included in *State Lines*, a book published by Texas A&M Press. He and his wife have two grown children.

[story behind the story]

"A Cigarette on the Champs-Élysées" was born during a period when newspapers were profitable, well-staffed news outlets. They had been my mainstay for most of my adult life, and I had worked at several. By the time I was chasing Ira Einhorn in France, I had worked my way up to the position of senior writer-at-large for the *Houston Chronicle*. It was an enviable position, one I thought was secure.

Ira Einhorn apparently enjoyed a similar sense of security, having thumbed his nose at authorities for years. Our worlds were shaken at about the same time, though for different reasons and in different ways. Years later, the irony of that came to me, along with the realization that almost all sense of security hangs by a thread.

Iris Podolsky

Iris Podolsky graduated cum laude from Rutgers University with a Bachelor of Arts degree in Romance Languages. She also holds a Master of Art in Art History.

She began her professional life teaching high school French, Spanish and English in Cranston, Rhode Island. Several business ventures followed her teaching career including interior design, medical office management and a wholesale showroom of women's accessories at the Dallas Apparel Mart. Throughout her life, Podolsky has pursued her passion for travel, music and food. She is a docent at the Dallas Museum of Art and an avid art collector.

[story behind the story]

Some women are either great in the bedroom or great in the kitchen. The women in my family have always been both. Stories of love and romance have circulated among us hot-blooded Hungarians for as long as I can remember. I was the surprise coming along after three much older sisters who often regaled me with tales of suitors and secret rendez-vous, love affairs and not-so-lovely affairs, told in the kitchen with lachen kugel in the oven. It was inevitable that at some point in my life, I would commit these rich, family sagas to paper.

My first effort came in 2009 with "Love and Lamb Chops," a bitter- sweet story about my father's death and mother's re-marriage, published in *Ten Spurs, The Best of the Best 2010*. I was only 10 when the story begins with Papa's fatal heart attack and 11 when my step-father began a furious campaign for Ma's hand. That led to a memoir focusing on my own quest for love and marriage. The resourceful young man I finally settled on will still not tell me how he arranged for his frat brother to stand me up so that he might take me out on that crucial first date. That was over 50 years ago. The manuscript, *In Full Bloom*, came under discussion at the Mayborn Conference in 2011.

"Red Stilettos," in 2012, centered around my sister, Lily, whose romance began with Ma's call to the butcher. "Mr. Katz, do you have any brains today?"

I'm now working on a novel, *The Lives and Loves of the Kugel Queens of Camden*, with overtones of our family's loves and losses set against the background of World War II. What else would I write about?

Sierra Mendez

Sierra Mendez is a recent graduate of the University of North Texas' College of Visual Arts & Design. She came to the Mayborn journalism program in her second year of graduate school because she missed words and the people who tell stories with them. Mendez lives in Denton, Texas, with her dog, Aurie, and her Apple computer, Bartholomew, whom she spends long hours staring at between fits of writing. Sierra has a bachelor's in English literature from Texas A&M University and works for the UNT College of Arts & Sciences as a Marketing & Publications Specialist.

[story behind the story]

It's really George's fault.

The story started as a one-shot – a brief narrative about Ethan's second trip to the barn to see Raine. I knew that it had the potential to be much bigger, but since my subject was six hours away during my last semester to work on my thesis, I was unsure about continuing working on it as a longer narrative.

George, however, was insistent.

The challenge I faced immediately – and what turned out to be the magic of this story, really – was that neither of my main characters could talk to me. I couldn't interview them. I couldn't ask them questions. I had to watch and learn and take the time to understand a language completely alien to me.

I also had to rely a great deal on the people around them for information and even interpretation of different behaviors and expressions.

What I realized is that I was learning a lot more about the people who surround Ethan than I was Ethan himself. What I realized I had was this friendship in the middle with something pure about it, something elemental, something untouched by agendas and motives and personal gain. And all around it was desperation and love and need and confusion.

I realized that, to do him justice, Ethan had to be portrayed in his own terms – in the physical presence that he is, without interpretations of his thoughts and relying instead on the motions of his shoulders, his mouth and his hands. And Raine was the same way.

My story is about their unique magic and their unique language.

Moira Muldoon

Moira Muldoon is a poet, columnist and essayist. She has written for *Wired.com*, *Salon*, *TechWeekly*, *Austin American-Statesman*, *American Way*, *D Magazine*, *Austin Chronicle*, *SFWeekly*, *GameSpot/ZDnet* and *videogames.com*. She's taught writing at Texas State University and Johns Hopkins University CTYOnline.

[story behind the story]

The deadline for the Mayborn essay contest came hard on the heels of my firewalking experience. I was pretty sure I wanted to submit an essay about firewalking; however, I usually like to think about essays for a while before I write them. And then write and rewrite them. But in order to make the Mayborn deadline, I had to think and rewrite faster than I was comfortable with. There was something freeing about that, something frankly joyful and fun. The piece had to stay more in the present than my essays usually do, had to be about action and impression, rather than reflection or rumination. Working on the piece over a single week, in between my regular paying gigs and taking care of the kids, forced me to use my rusty on-deadline journalism skills, such as they are, at the same time as my slower essay-writing skills.

Constraints can mean liberation for a writer – especially when said writer knows an editor will take a hard look to her piece before publication. As it turns out, it was a lucky thing that there was so little time for me between the experience and the writing.

Penne Richards

Penne Lynne Richards is a certified medical staff recruiter at UMC Health System in Lubbock, Texas. She enjoys making new acquaintances, believes a good interview is an art form, and strives to enhance her skills with each new opportunity. Penne takes pleasure in giving voice to those stories that need to be told – of people who exhibit extraordinary faith and will, with whom all can identify. She is drawn to motivating narratives that inspire and remind us of our limitless potential for strength and achievement.

When not working or writing, she enjoys lacing up her running shoes or hopping on her road bike to unwind. If traveling isn't an option, escaping into a good book is the next best thing. A graduate of Texas Tech University, Richards lives in Lubbock with her husband and the youngest of her three children.

[story behind the story]

I stood in the unusually crowded airport terminal in Lubbock, Texas, caught up in the excitement of the people around me. It was February 27, 2003, and most of those anxiously waiting consisted of family and friends of Angie Romans, a fun-loving friend I had met at work. I was there to support her – one mother to another. Angie was returning home from Beirut, Lebanon, newly reunited with her daughters kidnapped by her ex-husband ten years earlier. The terminal resembled a welcome party fit for a soldier returning home after a long tour of duty. American flags were being waved, welcome home banners were held high, and the local television reporters and cameramen filled in the gaps.

Perhaps it was during that visit to the airport that the idea of telling Angie's story, and that of her daughters', began a slow fire inside me. My dream was to one day get back to writing, my initial college major and passion until life took a different path. Writing, in some variation has always brought me great satisfaction. Years later, I learned of Angie's desire to find a writer to author a book detailing her story to leave a legacy for her family. I was moved by her ability to turn her will over to God and seek His tender mercies to heal her broken heart. I wanted to give voice to Angie's strength to face each morning, the courage to battle for her family and eventually impart her faith to her daughters. More time passed before I could build my own courage to believe I could write her story, and even longer before I approached Angie with the idea. Fortunately for me, she enthusiastically agreed. This for me was a dream fulfilled. As I worked on her story, I struggled with how to do justice to the events of her life but was inspired by the enormous hurdles she faced and overcame.

Angie and I became fast friends. Often we spent time indulging in many of the same outdoor pursuits – running, cycling, swimming and working out – and it was during those occasions I became captivated by her story. Over time, I learned more about her daughters and the struggles they faced during their journey to reunite. Passionate about the miracle God had performed, Angie was an open book and readily shared her memories. As I became more acquainted with her daughters, they gave me full access to interview them together and individually – through in-person visits, emails, texting and Skype chatting. I learned the details and the recollections of the kidnapping and their time in Lebanon. What I found riveting was their open discussions about the things they missed about Lebanon, the struggles they encountered and the reliance on their mother's faith to maintain hope. I listened with a mother's heart and ached at the pain of the separation they endured. Ultimately, theirs is a story of faith, courage and the power of a mother's love.

This essay is part of a larger work.

Pamela Skjolsvik

Given the choice between making the reader think or making the reader laugh, Pamela Skjolsvik prefers the latter. It hasn't been an easy trick during the past four years since she's been writing a book about death, but she did manage to sneak in a few laughs at her own expense. Skjolsvik received her MFA in Creative Nonfiction from Goucher College and has been published in *Creative Nonfiction*, *Ten Spurs* and *Witness* and she blogs regularly at www.thedeathwriter.blogspot.com.

[story behind the story]

What can I say? I needed a job and desperate times called for desperate measures. Working in a correctional facility wasn't a completely "out there" situation for me. My older brother was in and out and eventually back in for a 20-year stretch of my life. While visiting him for two hours at Folsom Prison was one thing, I realized that working a 12-hour shift in a small town jail was something else entirely. Naively, I approached my new job as though I was above my coworkers, but as the days passed, I discovered that institutionalization happens on both sides of the bars, and I was not immune to it.

The Staff

George Getschow

Editor

George Getschow, director and writer-in-residence of the nationally acclaimed Mayborn Literary Nonfiction Conference, spent 16 years at *The Wall Street Journal* as a reporter, editor, bureau chief, and on the Page One Rewrite Desk. At the *Journal*, he was a finalist for the Pulitzer Prize and won the Robert F. Kennedy Award for "distinguished writing" about the underprivileged. He covered Mexico for several years and directed the newspaper's coverage of the Southwest. Many of his protégés have won Pulitzer Prizes and other literary achievements. Today, he is a principal lecturer and writing coach for the Mayborn Graduate Institute of Journalism, and a writing coach for a number of storytellers in the Southwest. He was recently inducted into the Texas Institute of Letters for his "distinctive literary achievement." He's editor of *Ten Spurs*, a collection of the best essays and narratives submitted to the Mayborn's national writing contest. *Ten Spurs, Vol. 4*, was recently selected a "Notable Special Issue" by Robert Atwan for his renowned anthology, *2011 Best American Essays*. He's completing a book, *Walled Kingdom*, for John Macrae Books, an imprint of Henry Holt and Co., which grew out of two narratives he wrote for *The Wall Street Journal*.

Bill Marvel

Associate Editor

Bill Marvel worked for newspapers, covering cops, courts, politics, the arts, and freelanced pieces for major magazines. His work has appeared in *Smithsonian, Horizon, American Way, American Heritage, D Magazine, 5280, Southwest Spirit,* and *TWA's Ambassador.* Bill contends he's been laboring in the trenches of journalism for almost 50 years to do what he really wanted to do: write books. Since then he's been scrambling to make up for lost time, with *Burning Ludlow*, a narrative history of the great 1913-14 Colorado coal strike, the bloodiest labor conflict in U.S. History; with *Islands of the Damned,* a Marine's account of the Pacific War co-authoring with R.V. Burgin; and most recently with *A Mighty Fine Road*, a history of the Rock Island Railroad to be published in 2012 by Indiana University Press.

Martha Stroud

Illustrator

Martha Stroud, illustrator and former feature page designer at the *San Antonio Express-News*, has spent years at Southern newspapers honing her artistic craft. After graduating in 1987 from the University of Tennessee in Knoxville with a Bachelor of Fine Arts in Illustration, Stroud worked as a feature page designer, illustrator and graphic artist at the now defunct *Knoxville Journal*. She later worked at the *Lexington Herald-Leader* and the *Asheville Citizen-Times*. At *The State*, a daily in Columbia, S.C, Stroud was part of a team that won the prestigious Society of Newspapers Design Award, first-place, for a special section on the Gullahs, descendants of African slaves who live on islands off South Carolina. She is a member of The Society of Children's Book Writers and Illustrators and now lives in Tennessee where she is an illustrator for a national newspaper chain.

Noah Bunn

Design & Production

Noah Bunn's love affair with putting ink on paper began one Saturday afternoon at his grandmother's kitchen table. With a bottle of rubber cement, a metal ruler, and a sharp X-Acto knife, he set to work on the first edition of his middle school's newspaper. Since then, he's helped launch a 100,000-circulation regional magazine, earned a journalism degree in Faulkner's backyard, and been named a Mayborn Scholar at The University of North Texas. As a student, he led an enterprise reporting project in East Texas and won top prizes for both newspaper and feature writing from the Society of Professional Journalists. After a short stint at *Southern Living* magazine, Noah landed back in Dallas as an associate editor at *Spirit*, Southwest Airlines' in-flight magazine and a consultant to The Mayborn School of Journalism at The University of North Texas.